17 Sept · 54

Dear Peggy –
You've made our visit to Venice the most
pleasant time we've had this summer. I'm delighted
we're off to Milan together; after that we'll miss you, &
look forward to a return.   Sincerely,
                              Helen Frankenthaler

To Peggy, who's transferred her light
from N.Y. to Venice, to the former's
infinite loss & the latter's infinite
gain.
                    Clement Greenberg

Au lit.
Les lis...

              André Pieyre de Mandiargues

                    23 - 9 · 54

Peggy Guggenheim A Celebration

Peggy Guggenheim

A Celebration

Karole P. B. Vail

with an essay by Thomas M. Messer

GUGGENHEIM MUSEUM

Published on the occasion of the exhibition
organized by Karole P. B. Vail:

Peggy Guggenheim: A Centennial Celebration
Solomon R. Guggenheim Museum
June 12–September 2, 1998

H U G O   B O S S is the sponsor of this
exhibition as part of its ongoing support of the
Solomon R. Guggenheim Foundation

Omaggio a Peggy Guggenheim
Peggy Guggenheim Collection
September 30, 1998 – January 10, 1999

⊖ **Lufthansa**
Global Partner of the
Solomon R. Guggenheim Foundation

The operations and programs of the Peggy Guggenheim
Collection are supported by:

INTRAPRESÆ COLLEZIONE GUGGENHEIM

Aermec	iGuzzini Illuminazione
Arclinea	Istituto Poligrafico e Zecca
Automotive Products Italia	dello Stato
Banca Antoniana Popolare	Leo Burnett
Veneta	Lubiam 1911
Barbero 1891	Luciano Marcato
Bisazza	Rex Built-In
DLW AG	Sàfilo Group
Gretag Imaging Group	Swatch
Gruppo 3M Italia	Wella
Gruppo Imation Italia	Zucchi–Bassetti Group

Management by Bondardo Comunicazione

ISBN 0-8109-6914-9 (hardcover)
ISBN 0-89207-206-7 (softcover)

Guggenheim Museum Publications
1071 Fifth Avenue
New York, New York 10128

Hardcover edition distributed by
Harry N. Abrams, Inc.
100 Fifth Avenue
New York, New York 10011

Design by Tsang Seymour Design, Inc.,
New York

Printed in Italy by Amilcare Pizzi

Photo credits: pages 16, 61 (top), 64, 65,
68, 71, 84 (bottom), 85, 89, 90 (right),
96–97, 103, 104–05, 122, Ellen Labenski;
18, 62, Sergio Martucci; 26, Gérard Blot,
© RMN; 35, 83, 86, 90 (left), 91, 93,
98 (left and right), 99, 101, 109, 115,
116, David Heald.

All works of art in the Peggy Guggenheim
Collection reproduced in color were
photographed by David Heald, except those
on pages 32, 61 (bottom), and 79, which
were photographed by Sergio Martucci.

FRONT COVER
Peggy Guggenheim, photographed around
1924 by Man Ray (detail). Private collection

BACK COVER
Jean Cocteau, drawing in Peggy
Guggenheim's third guest book, 1956
(detail). Private collection

FRONTISPIECE
Peggy Guggenheim, photographed around
1940 by Rogi André (detail). Bibliothèque
Nationale de France, Paris, Département
des Estampes et de la Photographie

In memory of my parents, Sindbad and Peggy Angela Vail

Contents

Sponsor's Statement

Peggy Guggenheim: A Celebration pays homage to the lifework of a unique woman. Like her uncle Solomon R. Guggenheim, whose initiative created the museum in New York, Peggy—with her uncompromising passion for art—laid a cornerstone for the international scope of the Guggenheim today.

When, in 1995, Hugo Boss and the Guggenheim Museum decided to enter into a partnership, a new model of sponsorship was born—a creative collaboration whose driving force is the continuous exchange of ideas and thoughts transcending borders.

Just as Peggy Guggenheim championed contemporary art, we have made it our goal to recognize and promote innovation in the arts by teaming up with the Guggenheim Museum in New York to establish the Hugo Boss Prize, a biennial award to an artist whose work represents a major aesthetic achievement or significant development in contemporary art. In this way, we feel connected to her spirit.

Peggy Guggenheim was more than a collector of contemporary art. She was a patron with esprit and unmistakable style. This book is illustrated with artworks from the renowned Peggy Guggenheim Collection and photographs that document her life. Also shown is a selection of pages from Peggy's guest books; the signatures and drawings on these pages are a remarkable record of the international art community that visited her during her years in Venice.

Published on the occasion of an exhibition with which we are proud to have been associated, *Peggy Guggenheim: A Celebration* offers a rare and inspiring experience.

HUGO BOSS

Foreword

Peggy Guggenheim was among the most important and original figures to play a role in the art of this century. The centennial of her birth provides the perfect occasion to consider her enduring influence on the Solomon R. Guggenheim Foundation, an entity that was founded independently but came to encompass her lasting heritage, the Peggy Guggenheim Collection.

For me, as for its many visitors, the Peggy Guggenheim Collection is an indelible aspect of the Venice experience. Peggy settled in this fabled city in the last part of an eventful and fascinating life. And, although she had lived with a stubborn independence, it was to the organization founded by her uncle, another towering, but altogether different, art patron, that she bequeathed her legacy—the extraordinary collection of Modern painting and sculpture she assembled and the palazzo on Venice's Grand Canal that houses it.

The Guggenheim Foundation was founded in 1937 to realize four basic objectives: the collection, preservation, interpretation, and presentation of objects of twentieth-century visual culture. The Peggy Guggenheim Collection was the first European venue for the Guggenheim, and the inspiration for the vision that has led to our more recent multinational expansion. With the Guggenheim Museum Bilbao and the Deutsche Guggenheim Berlin, both of which opened to the public in the fall of 1997, the Guggenheim has solidified its international presence.

My predecessor as director of the Guggenheim, Thomas M. Messer, played a pivotal role in bringing the Peggy Guggenheim Collection into the Guggenheim Foundation. Though this event may seem, from our vantage, to have been preordained, in fact it was anything but. (For a chronicle of the complex story behind the bequest, see "The History of a Courtship" in this volume.) Under Tom's direction, the Peggy Guggenheim Collection and the Palazzo Venier dei Leoni were fully professionalized, through physical improvements and the development of a dedicated museum staff; in time, a program of temporary exhibitions was introduced to complement the permanent collection. In 1993, the palazzo and its garden were renovated and the museum enlarged to include a neighboring two-story building.

While special exhibitions have given the institution an added luster, it is Peggy's collection that continues to serve as the institution's greatest draw, luring some 250,000 visitors annually. The collection, however, has been augmented through extended loans of Modern and contemporary sculpture from the Patsy R. and Raymond D. Nasher Collection, and early twentieth-century Italian art from the Gianni Mattioli Collection. With a new tradition of development and growth, the future of the Peggy Guggenheim Collection promises to be as bright as its past.

It is that illustrious past that is so elegantly captured in this volume, published on the occasion of an exhibition mounted first at the Solomon R. Guggenheim Museum and then at the Peggy Guggenheim Collection. The show and this book are the result of several years of research by Peggy's granddaughter Karole P. B. Vail, a Project Curatorial Assistant at the Guggenheim. With her access to rare pieces, she has brought together a range of materials that tells the story of Peggy Guggenheim from an original perspective. Among the treasures exhibited to the public for the first time are childhood portraits of Peggy by Franz von Lenbach and Peggy's astonishing guest books. In these books, which she kept in her palazzo, scores of major cultural figures—such as John Cage, Jean Cocteau, Marcel Duchamp, Clement Greenberg, and Man Ray—wrote personal comments and poems and, in many cases, sketched charming drawings as mementos of their visits. A selection of pages from these guest books, which are still in family hands, are published in this volume for the first time.

The exhibition has been sponsored in New York by Hugo Boss, a long-term and valued partner of the Guggenheim Museum, and in Venice by Lufthansa German Airlines. The generous support of these two enlightened institutions continues to make possible so much of what the Guggenheim does.

Thomas Krens
Director
The Solomon R. Guggenheim Foundation

Acknowledgments

Peggy Guggenheim: A Centennial Celebration and its accompanying publication are dedicated to my late parents, Sindbad and Peggy Angela Vail. I am especially grateful to my mother, who initiated this project, and whose memory has been a constant inspiration to me.

This exhibition is the fruit of encouragement from family, friends, and colleagues, whom I hope will be as pleased with the result as I was in realizing it. I am fortunate to have benefited from their good humor and support, which has truly made this an enjoyable and invaluable experience for me.

At the Guggenheim, I am most grateful to my cousin Peter Lawson-Johnston, Chairman, for his constant support and enthusiasm, and to Thomas Krens, Director, who from the beginning advocated this important celebration of Peggy Guggenheim in the year of her centennial birthday. I am also deeply appreciative of the encouragement and advice of Lisa Dennison, Deputy Director and Chief Curator, Carmen Giménez, Curator of Twentieth-Century Art, and Judith Cox, Deputy Director and General Counsel.

I am particularly grateful for the assistance and insight of J. Fiona Ragheb, Assistant Curator, who spent many hours advising me on curatorial and editorial matters. I would also like to offer my appreciation to Jennifer Blessing, former Associate Curator, who keenly supported an exhibition on the "grande dame du Surréalisme."

Many other Guggenheim Museum staff members contributed enormously to the success of the exhibition. I am deeply grateful to Jodi Myers, Assistant Registrar, who skillfully handled the many complexities of the exhibition with constant good will and humor, and to Suzanne Quigley, Head Registrar for Collections and Exhibitions, for her assistance and enthusiasm. I also thank Karen Meyerhoff, Director of Exhibition and Collection Management and Design, for her talent and imagination, and Jocelyn Groom and Sean Mooney, Exhibition Design Coordinators.

I am immensely appreciative of the expertise of Gillian McMillan, Senior Conservator (Collections), and her talented team, including Eleonora Nagy, Associate Conservator for

Sculpture, and Nicole Basso, Conservation Coordinator. To Jocelyn Brayshaw, Chief Preparator for Paper, and to Elizabeth Jaff, Associate Preparator for Paper, I express my thanks for the superb presentation of the guest book pages and the photographs in the exhibition. Many thanks are also due to Alissa Warshaw, freelance mount maker and art handler, who beautifully designed the presentation of the earrings. I am very grateful to Peter Read, Manager of Fabrication and Design, and his crew, David Johnson, Chief Frame Maker, Scott Wilhelme, Cabinet Maker, and Stephen Engelman, Fabrication Technician. The organization of the installation was achieved through the contributions of Scott Wixon, Manager of Art Services and Preparations, Richard Gombar, Construction Manager, Anthony Villamena, Assistant Construction Manager, and Jonathan Welten and Bart Bettencourt under the supervision of Michael Sarff; Jeffrey Clemens, Art Handler, who oversaw the installation; and Mary Ann Hoag, Lighting Technician, who devised the exhibition's subtle lighting.

Deserving special thanks are my close neighbors on the third floor of the Guggenheim Museum SoHo, especially Vivien Greene, Curatorial Coordinator for Research and Exhibitions, who advised me on many matters, and Janice Yang, Project Research Exhibition Assistant. I would also like to thank Robert Rosenblum, Curator of Twentieth-Century Art, Nancy Spector, Curator of Contemporary Art, Matthew Drutt, Associate Curator for Research, Ilene Magaras, Librarian and Archivist, and particularly Ward Jackson, former Archivist, for their helpful guidance.

For their successful efforts to publicize the exhibition, I offer thanks to Scott Gutterman, Director of Public Affairs, Julia Caldwell, Public Affairs Coordinator, and Joyce Lee, Public Affairs Assistant.

My very special thanks go to Susan Madden, Director of Membership, who helped me decipher countless signatures in the guest books, and whose unfailing support was merely one of many facets of her friendship.

I am deeply indebted to David Heald, Chief Photographer and Director of Photographic Services, and his wonderful team, particularly Ellen Labenski, Assistant Photographer, for their photographs used for the exhibition and catalogue, and Kim Bush, Photography and Permissions Associate. I also thank Lee Ewing, former Assistant Photographer, for having photographed and documented the guest books.

The publication of this handsome and elegant book would not have been possible without the encouragement, generosity, and enthusiasm of Anthony Calnek, Director of Publications. I will be forever grateful to Edward Weisberger, Editor, for his meticulous and painstaking editing; Elizabeth Levy, Managing Editor/Manager of Foreign Editions, Esther Yun, Assistant Production Manager, and Melissa Secondino, Production Assistant, whose efforts ensured the beauty of this catalogue; and Carol Fitzgerald, Associate Editor, and Nicole Columbus, for their editorial thoroughness. I am delighted to have worked with Patrick Seymour and Ji Lee, Tsang Seymour Design Inc., New York, who designed the book with exceptional sensitivity. I also thank Susan Lee, Assistant Graphic Designer, who designed the exhibition's graphics; and Andrea Smalley, Membership Coordinator, and Peggy Allen, Development Assistant, who organized the opening event.

It has been a great honor to include in this catalogue the insightful essay of Thomas Messer, Director Emeritus, whose constant interest and support have been invaluable to this project.

I express my gratitude to Ruth Taylor, Director of Budgeting and Planning, Peter Katz, Budget Analyst, Ben Hartley, Director of Communications, and George McNeely, former Director of Corporate and Foundation Giving. I also thank Marilyn JS Goodman, Director of Education, Diane Maas and Felicia Liss, Education Program Managers, and Adele Kandel, Volunteer Coordinator.

To all the staff at the Peggy Guggenheim Collection, Venice, and in particular Philip Rylands, Deputy Director, I extend my thanks for the extraordinary support, advice, and understanding that enabled so many works of art to leave their home and reach more tumultuous American shores. My heartfelt thanks also go to Fred Licht, Curator; Renata Rossani, Administrator, for her myriad efforts; Paul Schwartzbaum, Chief Conservator, Guggenheim Museums/Technical Director, International Projects, for his unfailing support; Chiara Barbieri, Deputy Director's Assistant, for her valuable efforts; and Beate Barner, Assistant for Development and Public Affairs. I am grateful to Claudia Rech, Membership and Special Events Officer; Siro de Boni, Maintenance; and Sandra Rossi, former Publications Assistant. Jane Rylands, who rescued the guest books from the rising Venetian tides and entrusted them to my father, Sindbad Vail, deserves my very special thanks.

I would like to extend my heartfelt gratitude to the exhibition's lenders. I would particularly like to thank my sister, Julia Vail, who has been so generous and patient with me. My deepest appreciation goes to Anne Dopffer and Lydie Fouilloux, Musée National de la Coopération Franco-Américaine, Blérancourt; Peter C. Sutton and Mary C. Schroeder, Wadsworth Atheneum, Hartford; Malcolm Rogers, Randi Hopkins, and Kim Pashko, Museum of Fine Arts, Boston; Jean-Pierre Angrémy, Philippe Arbaïzar, and Hélène Fauré, Bibliothèque Nationale de France, Paris; Giandomenico Romanelli and Stefania Moronato, Civici Musei Veneziani d'Arte e di Storia; Helaine Pardo, Commerce Graphics Ltd, Inc., East Rutherford, New Jersey; Robert Gurbo, Estate of André Kertész, New York; Rona Roob, Claire Dienes, Charles Silver, and Ronald S. Magliozzi, the Museum of Modern Art, New York; Virginia M. Dortch; Kathy McCarver and Steven Mnuchin; and Ron Warren and Joshua Mack.

For providing me with the essential materials for the exhibition, I express my gratitude to Aube Breton Elléouët; Joanna Bruno, AP/Wide World Photos, New York; Gabriella Cardazzo; Gabriella Cecchini, Archivio Storico delle Arti Contemporanee, La Biennale di Venezia; Lillian Kiesler; Archivio Giuseppe Marchiori; Roloff Beny Collection, Documentary Art and Photography Division, National Archives of Canada, Ottawa; Mary Morel, *Life Magazine*, New York; Giorgio Santuzzo, Cameraphoto, Venice; Michael Stier, UPI/Corbis-Bettmann, New York; and especially my aunt Clover Vail.

I am more than grateful to the following people who have helped and encouraged me in my research: Giorgio Albertazzi; Bruno Alfieri; Sir Hardy Amies; Dore Ashton; Vittorio Barattolo; Luca Massimo Barbero; Will Barnet; Paolo Barozzi; Timothy Baum; Alberico Belgiojoso, Architetti BBPR, Milan; Louise Bourgeois; Gilberte Brassaï; Carolyn Brown; Art Buchwald; Andrea Bundonis; Richard Calvocoressi and Ann Simpson, Scottish National Gallery of Modern Art, Edinburgh; Giovanni Carandente; Gabriella Cardazzo; Renato Cardazzo; Sandra Carnielli; Sir Anthony Caro; Vittorio Carrain; Leonora Carrington; Lucy Carrington and Susan Train, *Vogue*, New York; Leo Castelli; Manop Charoensuk; Pierluigi Consagra; Pietro Consagra; Egidio Costantini and his family; Crosby Coughlin, Lorraine Mead, and Charles D. Scheips, Jr., Condé Nast Publications, New York; Mary Sharp Cronson; Sharon Daliana;

Robert Dance; Maxwell Davidson; André Emmerich; Amy Ernst; Dallas Ernst; Meredith Etherington-Smith, Christie's, London; Deborah Evetts; Claire Falkenstein; Felix Fertig; Stefano Fiuzzi; Charles Henri Ford; Helen Frankenthaler; Ann Freedman, Knoedler & Co. Galleries, New York; Milton Gendel; Kay Gimpel; Alexia Goethe; Karen Gravelle; Jenny Greenberg; Sir Alec Guinness; Yvonne Hagen; Anne d'Harnoncourt, Philadelphia Museum of Art; Shoshana Hasson; Seamus Heaney; Jacqueline Hélion; my cousin Nicolas Hélion; Maren Henderson; Kimbell Higgs; Al Hirschfeld; Lisa Hodgkin, *Vogue*, London; John Hohnsbeen; The Honorable Simon Howard; Sam Hunter; Lisa Jacobs; Buffie Johnson; Eric Kaufman; Nora Kennedy and Peter Mustardo, The Better Image, Pittstown, New Jersey; Lillian Kiesler; Monica Kinley; Leon Klayman; Sylvia Koner; Evelyn Lambert; Axel Lapp; James Lord; Luce Marinetti; Marina Marini; Georges Mathieu; Maria Gaetana Matisse; Jacqueline Matisse Monnier; Germana Matta Ferrari and Matta; Elizabeth Mayer; James Mayor; David McConnaughey; Jim Moon; Guy Mortimore; Robin Muir; Haya Murray; Jonathan Novak; Antony Penrose; Christopher Philips, *The New York Times*; Sir Norman Reid; Barbara Reis; Paul Resika; John Richardson; Steven Robeson-Miller; Ned Rorem; Michael Rosenfeld, Michael Rosenfeld Gallery, New York; my cousins Laurence and Sandro Rumney; John Russell; Michelangelo Sabatino; Shojii Sadao and Amy Hau, the Isamu Noguchi Foundation, Inc., Long Island City; Ben Schneiderman; Charles Seliger; Sally Sloan, Fundación Robert Brady, A. C., Cuernavaca; Lord Snowdon; Matthew Spender; Maureen St.-Onge; Leo Steinberg; Saul Steinberg; Hedda Sterne; Jane Strong; Roger Straus; David Sylvester; Lucien Treillard; my aunt Kathy Vail; Catherine Vare, Christie's, New York; Gore Vidal; Jacqueline Weld; Kirk Winslow; Judith Young-Mallin; and Daniela Zamburlin, *Il Gazzettino*.

I offer my friends, and in particular M., my heartfelt gratitude and affection for the forbearance and constant support they gave me. I hope that some day I may do the same for them.

Karole P. B. Vail

Peggy Guggenheim: Life and Art

Karole P. B. Vail

The Guggenheims

A little girl with long locks of hair clutches her hands tightly.
She stands in an awkward but determined way, looking out
directly and inquisitively. Her big eyes sparkle. Her pert mouth
quivers slightly. She dares not move lest the painter reprimand
her. Around 1903, Franz von Lenbach, a German artist
favored by Bavarian high society, painted my grandmother
Peggy Guggenheim "for some strange reason" with "brown eyes
instead of green, and red hair instead of chestnut."[1] Though
later Peggy would not favor figurative art, she cherished this formal portrait—whose date she had erased so that people would
not guess her age—and, even more, the portrait, also by
Lenbach, of herself and her older sister, Benita, who with her
beautiful brown hair and brown eyes did not need fanciful
embellishments. As befitted a man of his position, her father, the
dashing Benjamin Guggenheim, had commissioned these paintings, which Peggy considered "the greatest treasures of my
past."[2] In later years, she kept them in her bedroom in Venice as
reminders of her childhood and of those days when her father
and sister were still alive.

On August 26, 1898, Peggy, the second of three daughters,
was born into two wealthy and famous New York Jewish families: the Guggenheims and the Seligmans. A half century before,
in 1848—a year of political turmoil throughout Europe—her
paternal grandfather, Simon Guggenheim, and his son, Meyer,
had left the ghetto of Lengnau in German Switzerland, and
sailed for Philadelphia, dreaming of success and freedom.
Indeed, Philadelphia and Pennsylvania were among the most
liberal of all the cities and states of the United States, as well
as being important political, cultural, and economic centers.
Father and son peddled household goods door-to-door, and

Franz von Lenbach
Benita and Peggy Guggenheim,
ca. 1903
Oil on board, 88.3 x 54.6 cm
Private collection

Meyer, taking full advantage of his newfound freedom, began to
manufacture stove polish, the first of many family industries—
which would come to include speculations in foodstuffs and
spices, and lace and embroidery manufacturing. The greatest
wealth, however, would come from investments in mining, especially lead and silver mines near Leadville, Colorado.

Meyer had seven sons and three daughters with his wife,
Barbara. She nurtured her children, placing an emphasis on culture and particularly on the appreciation of music. Meyer disciplined each son to ensure that they would work hard and stay
together. He said that together the brothers were as strong as a
bundle of sticks, but apart they were as weak as a single stick,
which could be easily broken. The brothers were all partners
in M. Guggenheim's Sons, the family-owned business. Benjamin,
born in 1865, was Meyer's sixth child and one of the younger
and wilder sons. Of the other brothers, Solomon would become
the founder of the Solomon R. Guggenheim Foundation and
of the Museum of Non-Objective Painting (the Solomon R.
Guggenheim Museum opened posthumously), and Simon would
establish the John Simon Guggenheim Memorial Foundation,
famous for its grants. Benjamin was sent to Leadville to learn
the mining business during his college summers; although he did
not graduate, he was the first of the Guggenheims to attend an
institution of higher learning. He became the manager of the
Philadelphia smelter in Pueblo, Colorado.

In 1888, Meyer and his wife moved from Philadelphia to New York's Upper West Side, and the sons soon followed. In 1894, Benjamin married Florette Seligman from the very successful international banking family. Joseph Seligman, the first of his family to come to America, had left the Bavarian village of Baiersdorf and arrived in 1837, a decade before the Guggenheims left Lengnau. All of his siblings, including five brothers, subsequently emigrated. James Seligman, Peggy's maternal grandfather, established a dry-goods store in New York in 1846, and he and the other brothers founded the banking firm of J. & W. Seligman in New York in 1864. The Seligmans— established in New York long before the Guggenheims moved there—were considered the more socially elite and cultivated of the two families. James and his wife, Rosa, had eight children, many of whom exhibited troubling eccentricities and ailments. Of Florette's two sisters, one sang rather than spoke her conversations and the other was catatonic. Florette herself repeated everything she said three times: "Shush, Peggy will see, Peggy will see, Peggy will see."[3] Benjamin was upset that his wife's family considered him their social inferior, and Florette's own behavior was perhaps so odd that he may have concluded he made a mistake when he married her. As Peggy recalled, "I guess she didn't attract him and other women attracted him more."[4] Not a good omen for a happy family. Indeed, he soon started having extramarital affairs, and continued to have them even after the births of three daughters: Benita, born in 1895; Peggy, who had been born Marguerite and called Maggie by her father; and Hazel, born in 1903.

Although Benjamin and William, the youngest brother, were the smelting experts of the family, neither was consulted in 1899 when the Guggenheim Exploration Company, known as Guggenex, was formed. Both brothers objected to the new corporate entity because, unlike M. Guggenheim's Sons, it welcomed outside investors. By that time, Benjamin had become quarrelsome at family meetings and was considered to be the black sheep of the Guggenheim family because of his personal indiscretions. Benjamin and William separated themselves from the family business, which subsequently became more cohesive in its organization. Among its widespread endeavors, Guggenex took control of the American Smelting and Refining Company and mining industries all over the world. By the beginning of World War I, the Guggenheims and their associates reportedly controlled between seventy-five and eighty percent of the world's silver, copper, and lead mines. Benjamin was to miss out on the grandest era of Guggenheim business expansion, and Florette and their daughters were to suffer the financial consequences.

After 1900, Benjamin dabbled in business enterprises in Paris and New York, but the earnings from his largely unsuccessful ventures paled beside the vast riches he would have gained had he stayed in Guggenex. He spent most of his time in Europe and took up residence in Paris, where he had numerous French mistresses. His traveling and philandering soon meant that he and Florette were man and wife in name only. He spent more and more of his time in Paris, where he invested in and worked for International Steam Pump, which had built the elevators for the Eiffel Tower.

In April 1912, Benjamin decided to sail back to New York with his latest mistress, a young singer; after passage on another vessel had been postponed, they embarked on the Titanic. The ship's fatal maiden voyage would soon enter history. Benjamin and his faithful secretary, Victor Giglio—apparently having given their life jackets to others—were dressed in evening clothes, ready to die as heroes. Benjamin gave one of the stewards, who was to man a lifeboat into which women and children were loaded, a last message for Florette: "Tell her that I played the game straight to the end and that no woman was left on board this ship because Ben Guggenheim was a coward."[5] The Titanic sank to the bottom of the sea, and over 1,500 passengers went to their deaths. The mistress, however, was saved and in a rather ironic twist was referred to in a list of passengers published in *The New York Times* as Mrs. Benjamin Guggenheim. Once their Guggenheim uncles cleared up Benjamin's muddled business affairs—a process that took seven years—each daughter inherited $450,000, which was placed in trust. Contrary to popular belief, Peggy never had unlimited funds, though she was never by any standards poor. She learned to use her wits, and the use she made of her income would be imaginative and inventive.

In many ways, Peggy never fully recovered from her father's death. She said that throughout her life she was searching to find in other men the beloved father she had lost too soon. Nonetheless, the relationship had not been a simple one. Peggy later summed up her feelings about him: "I adored my father because he was fascinating and handsome, and because he loved me. But I suffered very much because he made my mother unhappy."[6] In order to understand Peggy, it is important to keep

Peggy Guggenheim, 1913.
Private collection

in mind that she grew up in an unstable and unhappy family.
Acutely aware of the alienation between their parents and placed
in the care of governesses, Peggy as well as her sisters Benita
and Hazel felt rejected. Even though there was no lack of tennis
parties, beautiful clothes, and exotic pet dogs, Peggy wrote,
"Not only was my childhood excessively lonely and sad, but it
was also filled with torments."[7] The love of Peggy's childhood was
her sister Benita, who served as substitute mother and best
friend. Their portrait by Lenbach conveys that sisterly love,
Peggy tenderly leaning against her sister's protective shoulder.

Peggy and her sisters were taught history, music, and literature by private tutors and governesses. From an early age, she
had been exposed to culture and to traveling in Europe, including
visits to museums. She had a "voracious appetite" for reading,[8]
which would be a lifelong passion. It was not until 1914 that
Peggy attended a formal learning institution, the Jacoby School,
a private school for Jewish girls in New York. After graduating in

1915,[9] she continued to study and was much influenced by one teacher in particular, Lucile Kohn, who "had a passion for bettering the world"[10] and taught her "about life, the poor and the needy, blacks and whites, etc."[11] Peggy wrote that it was thanks to Kohn that she "became radical and finally emerged from the stifling atmosphere in which I had been raised."[12] This break with her sheltered past would become more pronounced when Peggy turned twenty-one in 1919, and thus gained direct control of the income from her trust. Subsequently, her gifts of "countless $100s" made it possible for Kohn to begin "a lifetime involvement with trade unions."[13]

After her birthday in 1919, Peggy celebrated her independence by traveling extensively in the United States. In the winter of 1920, "being very bored," Peggy, wishing for "a nose 'tip-tilted like a flower,' something I had read about in Tennyson,"[14] went to Cincinnati for a nose operation. The operation was not a success, and "every time it rained, I knew it beforehand, because my nose became a sort of barometer and would swell up in bad weather."[15] Shortly afterward, Peggy's admittedly frivolous preoccupations took a more serious turn when Margaret Anderson, editor and publisher of *The Little Review*—the avant-garde magazine in which James Joyce's *Ulysses* was first published in America—asked for a donation: "She said that if people believed in preventing wars the best possible thing to do was to subscribe to the arts."[16] In youthful innocence, Peggy gave five hundred dollars to *The Little Review*, hoping to have put off the next world war for several years. This naive gesture was probably Peggy's first financial contribution in favor of the arts. It is interesting to note the influence that independent women, such as Anderson and Kohn, had in her life from this early stage. These women introduced her to the arts and social issues; they encouraged her liberation of spirit and mind and a new social awareness.

In 1920, Peggy temporarily substituted for her dentist's nurse. The experience—something quite extraordinary and unheard of for a young woman in her social position—left her feeling "in need of a job."[17] Peggy went to work for her cousin Harold Loeb, who was a coowner of Sunwise Turn, a radical bookshop located near Grand Central Terminal; the store also exhibited art. Loeb was the real-life inspiration for the character Robert Cohn in Ernest Hemingway's *The Sun Also Rises* (1926). An enthusiastic, energetic, and eager worker, Peggy took care of the bookkeeping. The catch was that she worked for free; in compensation, she received a discount on any books she purchased: "In order to have the illusion of receiving a big salary, I bought many books of modern literature and read them all with my usual voracity."[18] Peggy's wealthy aunts came to buy books by the yard for their bookshelves at home. The bookshop was frequented by celebrated artistic and literary personalities, and there Peggy met Marsden Hartley; Leon Fleischman and his wife, Helen; and the flamboyant, blond-haired Laurence Vail. An artist and writer, Vail shocked, fascinated, and quite overwhelmed Peggy with his freedom. The Fleischmans introduced her to the art dealer and photographer Alfred Stieglitz, who showed her a Georgia O'Keeffe canvas, the first abstract painting that Peggy ever saw.

Laurence Vail: The King of Bohemia

After working at Sunwise Turn for six months, Peggy sailed to Europe, ostensibly for a visit, but she would end up living in France and England until the summer of 1941. In Paris, she again met Laurence Vail, who "was considered the King of Bohemia,"[19] and it would be he who most changed Peggy's life in her early adult years—for better and for worse. Laurence, a more serious man than Peggy has described in her memoirs, had lived most of his life in France, where he was born in 1891 to American parents. His father, Eugene Vail, was a painter, and Laurence, who studied English literature at Oxford University, wrote plays and articles, translated books from French into English, painted, and made extraordinary collages and sculptures. Peggy and Laurence's romance flourished in Paris, and he proposed to her at the top of the Eiffel Tower. They married in 1922, and while honeymooning in Capri they were joined by Laurence's sister, Clotilde, who traveled with them through Italy to Saint Moritz. Peggy found that she had married into a family as strange as her own. Laurence "was locked in a lifelong alliance with his sister which had been formed in childhood against their cold martinet of a mother with her chilly New England soul and their neurotic father."[20] Given the intensity of the relationship between Laurence and Clotilde, Peggy considered her "the thorn in my marriage,"[21] and their relationship would always be difficult.

In many ways, Peggy and Laurence complemented each other. Laurence was not Jewish, and he "was a veritable soul of wit. Constantly amazed at life's contradictions, he was forever

Laurence Vail.
Collection of Clover Vail

alert to the absurd. He was worldly, ironic, sophisticated, mischievous, and no fool, although utterly impractical about money."[22] His background and social circle were totally at odds with the family and Jewish society that Peggy had left behind in New York. To Laurence, Peggy was a young woman to whom he could teach art, literature, and life. She also had money, and this was no small attraction for him, particularly as he had always relied on the monthly checks his mother sent him. Perhaps inevitably, Laurence's passionate, at times violent, nature and Peggy's inexperience and immaturity were not conducive to a happy marriage. Quickly, husband and wife began to quarrel, and the years with Laurence would be tumultuous.

Paris in the 1920s was the center of an intense intellectual, artistic, and social life. Writers and artists haunted the tables of such Montparnasse cafés as Le Dôme and, just across the way, La Rotonde. Laurence spent hours sitting in cafés with Clotilde, drinking, talking, looking, and being looked at. Djuna Barnes, Mary Reynolds—two women who, according to Peggy, "had the kind of nose I had gone all the way to Cincinnati for in vain"[23]— *The New Yorker* art critic Robert Coates, Marcel Duchamp, Man Ray, and writer and publisher Robert McAlmon were just some of the friends, including many expatriate Americans, with whom Peggy and Laurence spent time during the day and at parties that went on all night. It is not surprising that this Parisian milieu had a significant effect on Peggy's growing artistic awareness. Years later, however, Peggy said that "perhaps I didn't like Paris in the twenties, everyone was drinking. I tried hard to be bohemian but I was really not convinced. . . . I have never smoked opium myself. I am too much of a puritan."[24] She was unconventional but had a practical personality. In contrast to her desire to shock people, she was always aware of her social position, of her American, albeit Jewish, upper-class background.

In 1923, my father, Sindbad Vail, was born in England, where Peggy and Laurence had gone for the birth so that their child, if male, could avoid the obligation of military service in France. When Peggy was thin again, she let herself be photographed by Man Ray in a glamorous gold-lamé evening dress designed by the famous couturier Paul Poiret. Captured in a sophisticated pose, she wears a headdress made by Vera Soudeikine, the longtime mistress and later wife of Igor Stravinsky. Laurence liked Peggy to dress extravagantly, and he himself was noted for his eccentric attire: shirts made from unusual fabrics as well as jackets and pants in bright colors.

In between wild parties and marital rows in Paris, trips to the Tyrol, to Italy, and even to Egypt were undertaken. What Peggy enjoyed most was "getting acquainted with Venice on foot. Laurence had lived there as a child for his father had always gone there in the autumn to paint. Laurence knew every stone, every church, every painting in Venice; in fact he was its second Ruskin. He walked me all over this horseless and autoless city and I developed for it a lifelong passion."[25]

During a trip to New York in 1925, Peggy—pregnant with her second child—arranged for the exhibition and sale in galleries and department stores of flower cut-outs by Mina Loy. Having returned to France, Peggy and Laurence departed for Switzerland, where a daughter, Pegeen, was born. Although this did not do much to tame Peggy's and Laurence's undomesticated spirits, they decided to live in the south of France in Pramousquier, near Le Lavandou. Their house, formerly an inn, had a particular appeal because Jean Cocteau and his lover Raymond Radiguet—who died in 1923—had stayed there. They had many visitors, including Peggy's cousin Harold Loeb, Loy and her two daughters, the Surrealist painter André Masson, Reynolds, and Clotilde.

The artist Alfred Courmes, who had become friends with Clotilde, spent time with all the Vails in Pramousquier as well as in Paris. As a token of his friendship, and grateful for the welcome he had received from them, he painted a classical and formal portrait of Peggy, with the Vails' car, a red Dietrich-Lorraine, and the Mediterranean in the background. However, it seems that Peggy did not much care for the portrait and decided not to acquire it.

Peggy and Laurence alternated between Paris and their country life in Pramousquier. Laurence worked on his novel *Murder! Murder!* (1931), a funny and hurtful satire of their life together. In 1925, Peggy undertook a retail venture with Loy, which apparently lasted into 1928. Peggy rented a shop—located on the chic rue du Colisée in Paris—that was set up to sell Loy's lamp bases and shades. In running the shop, Peggy discovered that she had a talent for business, but Loy found the experience stifling and stressful.

Man Ray's talented assistant Berenice Abbott, wanting to strike off on her own, borrowed money from Peggy to set up her own photography studio in 1926. A grateful Abbott repaid the debt by taking lovely photographs of Peggy sporting fashionably short hair, wearing exotic earrings and bright lipstick, and

FACING PAGE

Alfred Courmes
Portrait of Peggy Guggenheim, 1926
Oil on canvas, 100 x 65 cm
Musée National de la Coopération Franco-Américaine, Château de Blérancourt,
Gift of the Amis du Musée, 1985

holding her small children or her dog. Abbott admired Peggy, whom she considered a person of genuine seriousness.

Life with John Holms

In the summer of 1927, Peggy learned of the second tragedy in her life when she inadvertently opened a telegram addressed to Laurence. In this abrupt manner, she found out that Benita had died in childbirth, and that her child was born dead too. Peggy never forgave herself for not having been with her sister in New York. She believed that a jealous Laurence had kept the sisters apart, and the couple's growing estrangement was exacerbated by the fact that Laurence resented Peggy's lengthy period of mourning for Benita.

That winter, Peggy met the anarchist Emma Goldman, and subsequently, in the summer of 1928, Goldman worked on her memoirs, entitled *Living My Life* (1931), in a house that Peggy provided for her in Saint-Tropez. Goldman's secretary, Emily Coleman, "a mad American girl"[26] passionately interested in people, literature, and life, was in love with John Holms, an English writer. He was greatly admired by Edwin Muir, who with his wife, Willa, translated the writings of Franz Kafka into English. Peggy was immediately attracted to Holms: "He had a magnificent physique. . . . and looked very much like Jesus Christ."[27] The evening that Peggy met Holms was on the first anniversary of Benita's death. The fateful kiss they gave each other—soon after Peggy had danced on a table in a Saint-Tropez bistro—marked the end of Peggy's marriage to Laurence. Some weeks later, Peggy and Holms ran off together. As part of the divorce settlement, it was agreed that Peggy should have custody of Pegeen and Laurence custody of Sindbad; the divorce itself was not final until 1930. Peggy and Laurence—who soon took up with, and later married, the novelist Kay Boyle—came to have a friendlier relationship as the years passed, and their children would spend considerable time visiting with each parent.

Peggy later acknowledged her debt to Holms: "During the five years that I lived with him, I began to learn everything I know today. When I first met him I was like a baby in a kindergarten, but by degrees he taught me everything and sowed the seeds in me that sprouted after he was no longer there to guide me."[28] In the spring of 1932, after an active life in Paris and much traveling throughout Europe, they settled in England, near Dartmoor in Devon. They lived at Hayford Hall, which was dubbed "Hangover Hall."[29] Djuna Barnes, the painter Louis Bouché and his family, Coleman, Wyn Henderson—Peggy's future assistant at Guggenheim Jeune—and the novelist Antonia White were among the frequent visitors. It was here that the talented, chic, and dynamic, but rather resentful, Barnes—to whom Peggy had been giving financial support—wrote her famous novel *Nightwood*, which she dedicated to Peggy and Holms when it was published in 1936. (Until Peggy died, she sent Barnes a monthly stipend, and Sindbad generously continued to do so until his own death.)

Holms—who could write brilliantly but whose promise was largely unfulfilled because he was unable to write a book—conversed with Peggy and their guests when he was not drinking heavily. The couple also spent much time in London. In January 1934, Holms died during what should have been a routine operation to reset a dislocated wrist. Apparently, the high level of alcohol in his blood combined with the anesthetic caused heart failure. Peggy had suddenly lost the man she would always consider the love of her life. She wondered if she could have prevented the deaths of those closest and dearest to her: first her father, then Benita, and now Holms. Regarding these

John Holms and Peggy Guggenheim with her children, Sindbad and Pegeen Vail, around 1930.
Private collection

deaths, her sense of helplessness was understandable. However, in situations during which she might have exercised genuine responsibility she often did not do so. Throughout Peggy's life, she tended to be least protective of those people to whom she had the most personal obligations, such as her lovers, children, or grandchildren.

Within a few months of Holms's death, Peggy began an affair with Douglas Garman, whom she had met and been attracted to while Holms was still alive. Garman, a fanatical Communist, worked as a publisher for a progressive publishing house in London. In a domestic fashion of sorts, in the summer of 1935, they began to live together in Yew Tree Cottage in the countryside, southwest of London, near the small town of Petersfield. In the spring of 1936, when the *International Surrealist Exhibition* opened at the New Burlington Galleries, Peggy refused—ironically in light of the way her life would soon develop—to go to London; the city still reminded her too much of Holms. For ten days in the summer, however, she did go to Venice. Years later, she wrote fondly of this trip, "I revisited all my favorite churches and museums, and felt the same delight I always had in [the Venetian Renaissance painter] Carpaccio."[30] Differing more and more over politics, and also because Garman refused to marry Peggy, the couple ended their relationship early in 1937.

Peggy Guggenheim and her children, Sindbad and Pegeen Vail, early 1930s. Private collection

Guggenheim Jeune

A turning point for Peggy occurred in May 1937, when her close friend Peggy Waldman wrote to her suggesting that she do something serious with her life, such as open an art gallery or establish a publishing house, "anything that would be engrossing yet impersonal."[31] Thinking that an art gallery would be a less expensive venture than a publishing house, she opted for the former little knowing how much energy and money she would pour into it. In true Guggenheim fashion, she liked the idea of becoming a patron of the arts—and perhaps also making a profit. Peggy's financial ability to start a gallery was strengthened by an inheritance from her mother, who died that November in New York.

Although Peggy's contacts had been mainly with literary figures, she quickly embraced the world of avant-garde art. Humphrey Jennings, then a Surrealist painter but later a filmmaker, helped her look for a gallery space in London. In Paris,

he introduced her to such Surrealists as André Breton, known
as the "Pope of Surrealism," and Yves Tanguy. The collaboration
with Jennings was short-lived, and Peggy hired her bright and
energetic friend Wyn Henderson as her assistant. It was
Henderson who decided to name the gallery Guggenheim Jeune,
a clever pun on the name of the famous gallery Bernheim Jeune
in Paris. Guggenheim Jeune was located at 30 Cork Street, in
the heart of Piccadilly.

Peggy knew virtually nothing about Modern art: "At that
time I couldn't distinguish one thing in art from another."[32]
Her personal taste had been largely for Renaissance art and the
Old Masters. In fact, she had read all of Bernard Berenson's
books and swore by his aesthetic principles. She turned to
Marcel Duchamp, a lover of her and Laurence Vail's friend Mary
Reynolds, for guidance. He taught Peggy the difference between
abstract and Surrealist art and introduced her to Jean Arp, Jean
Cocteau, and many other artists. The charismatic Duchamp

31

had become a legend when his controversial painting *Nude Descending a Staircase No. 2* (1912, Philadelphia Museum of Art) was exhibited at the 1913 Armory Show in New York. Having previously advised the American collectors Louise and Walter Arensberg and Katherine Dreier, Duchamp was happy to counsel Peggy on her future purchases. It is to Peggy's credit that she was wise enough to diligently follow the advice of Duchamp and later advisers.

Peggy wanted to devote the first Guggenheim Jeune exhibition to Constantin Brancusi, but the sculptor was not in Paris when Peggy came over to make arrangements. Duchamp suggested an exhibition of works by Cocteau, whom Peggy duly visited in his opium-scented hotel room in Paris. Duchamp also introduced her to Arp, "an excellent poet and a most amusing man."[33] She fell in love with his brass sculpture *Head and Shell* (ca. 1933): "The instant I felt it I wanted to own it."[34] It was to be the first artwork to enter Peggy's collection.

Through her old friend Helen Fleischman, now married to James Joyce's son, Giorgio, Peggy was introduced to Samuel Beckett in December 1937. He fascinated her, and she talked with him about literature and art. When Peggy admitted to Beckett that she preferred Old Master paintings, he strongly encouraged her to accept and encourage the art of their day, "as it was a living thing."[35] In addition to his passion for Joyce, he admired the painters Jack Yeats (brother of William Butler Yeats) and Geer van Velde. An odd relationship—more of a strange sexual friendship than a truly amorous affair—ensued

Jean Arp
Head and Shell (Tête et coquille), ca. 1933
Polished brass, 19.7 cm high
Peggy Guggenheim Collection
76.2553 PG 54

with Beckett, who liked liberated women. Peggy ultimately
found him to be too passive and eccentric; she nicknamed him
"Oblomov" after the neurotic, indolent hero of Ivan Goncharov's
1858 novel. She certainly did not, and perhaps could not, fathom
this complex intellectual, and she infringed too much on his
privacy. Peggy was undoubtedly in love with Beckett in her own
erratic way, and they went on seeing each other from time to
time during the remainder of the late 1930s.

Peggy's life was hectic; she divided her time between Paris
and London, particularly because of the arrangements being
made for Cocteau's exhibition (January 24–February 12, 1938).
The exhibition would include drawings and furniture designed
for his play *Les Chevaliers de la Table Ronde*, which had
opened in Paris in October 1937, as well as other drawings and
objects. One of two drawings on linen bedsheets, which included
a portrait of Jean Marais—who acted in the play and was a
recent discovery of Cocteau's—caused a scandal with British customs inspectors; they objected to the depiction of pubic hair,
which had been modestly pinned over with a few leaves.
This piece was released on the condition that it not be exhibited

Marcel Duchamp, photographed in 1930
by Man Ray.
The Young Mallin Archive, New York,
V. Thomson Papers

to the general public, and Peggy only showed it to a few people in private. Beckett translated Cocteau's catalogue text into English. The exhibition opened to great fanfare, but without Duchamp, who did not attend openings, and without a hospitalized Beckett, who sent a telegram of congratulations to a jubilant Peggy. Simultaneously in Paris, the huge 1938 *International Exhibition of Surrealism* was being held, and reports of its wild opening were linked to Peggy's opening, much to her delight.

Peggy continued to let herself be guided in a docile fashion by Duchamp, on whose recommendation she exhibited the abstract work of Vasily Kandinsky (February 18–March 12); it was his first solo exhibition in England. Kandinsky had formerly enjoyed good fortune with Solomon Guggenheim, who, together with his wife, Irene, and his artistic adviser, Hilla Rebay, had visited the artist in his studio in Dessau in 1929. On this occasion, Solomon had bought his first oil painting by Kandinsky, an abstraction entitled *Composition 8* (1923). Rebay encouraged Solomon to collect Kandinsky's work. Destined to become the first director of the Museum of Non-Objective Painting (which would open in 1939 and be renamed the Solomon R. Guggenheim Museum in 1952), she enthusiastically embraced the art of her time. Herself a painter, she was passionately interested in nonobjective painting, believing that it was infused with spirituality. By 1938, however, Kandinsky, once supported so fiercely, had been supplanted by the lesser artist Rudolf Bauer, who was now greatly favored by an enamored Rebay.

The Guggenheim Jeune exhibition of Kandinsky works from 1909 to 1937 had a catalogue that included a preface by André Breton, the Surrealist artist that Kandinsky felt closest to. Peggy wrote to Solomon offering to sell to him, at Kandinsky's insistence, an early work that he had apparently once desired. This prompted Rebay's wrath; she believed that Peggy was slandering her family's good name: "It is extremely distasteful at this moment, when the name of Guggenheim stands for an ideal in art, to see it used for commerce," she wrote to Peggy.[36] To a third party, Rebay observed, "Peggy Guggenheim is trying to ride on our fame," but finished on a more positive note, "however, I believe it can do only good if she buys lots of paintings of the poor starving painters in times like this."[37] Solomon did not buy a Kandinsky from his niece, but in 1945 he acquired *Dominant Curve* (April 1936) from the German dealer Karl Nierendorf; Peggy, who had bought the painting from her Kandinsky exhibition, later regretted that she had sold it to Nierendorf.

Vasily Kandinsky
Dominant Curve (Courbe dominante),
April 1936
Oil on canvas, 129.4 x 194.2 cm
Solomon R. Guggenheim Museum 45.989

An exhibition of celebrity portraits by Cedric Morris (March 18–April 7) was followed by *Exhibition of Contemporary Sculpture* (April 8–May 2), which was proposed by Duchamp. Arp helped Duchamp with the selection, which was made up of works by Arp, Brancusi, Alexander Calder, Raymond Duchamp-Villon, Henri Laurens, Henry Moore, Antoine Pevsner, and Sophie Taeuber-Arp. Much of the sculpture was shipped from Paris, and more problems with British customs ensued. James B. Manson, director of the Tate Gallery, London, refused to certify the sculptures as art, thus subjecting them to import duties. A petition was signed by art critics, and finally the House of Commons voted to let the works in duty-free. Manson left his post shortly thereafter. By the time the exhibition opened, it was already famous, much to Peggy's delight and credit. Further, the presence of Arp, a cofounder of Dada, was particularly invigorating for British artists. Moore was thrilled to be shown "alongside other European sculptors"[38] and always grateful to Peggy for the opportunity. The London art scene had been sleepy in comparison with that of Paris, but there were now such galleries as the Mayor Gallery and the London Gallery, Peggy's neighbors on Cork Street. The London Gallery, owned by the wealthy writer, painter, and collector Roland Penrose, was directed by E. L. T. Mesens, editor of *London Bulletin*, the official forum of the British Surrealists. Mesens arranged to run off copies of catalogues for exhibitions held at the Cork Street galleries. Penrose and the poet David Gascoyne were largely responsible for encouraging Surrealism in London. Their efforts led in 1936 to the *International Surrealist Exhibition* at the New Burlington Galleries. The exhibition was a succès de scandale, spurred on by the defiant catalogue introduction written by art historian Herbert Read, who would become an important figure in Peggy's life.

Guggenheim Jeune became a catalyst in the growing appreciation for Modern art in England. The gallery's first season included a solo exhibition, which had been proposed by Beckett, of paintings and gouaches by his friend van Velde (May 5–26). Next came two simultaneous solo exhibitions of works by Benjamin Benno, a friend of Pablo Picasso, and Rita Kernn-Larsen (May 31–June 18). These were followed by *Exhibition of Contemporary Painting and Sculpture* (June 21–July 2), which showed works by such British artists as Eileen Agar, Edward Burra, and Paul Nash alongside others by continental artists such as Max Ernst, Kandinsky, and René Magritte. This was the first time Peggy exhibited Ernst, but they would not actually meet until winter 1938–39. On the advice of Jennings, the season ended with a solo exhibition of paintings by Tanguy (July 6–16). It was "beautifully hung and looked wonderful,"[39] as well as being, for the first time in the gallery's brief history, a small financial success. Peggy found the married Tanguy to be adorable and funny; inevitably, an intense affair between patron and artist ensued. For Peggy, Tanguy painted two miniatures for earring settings; Read said these were "the best Tanguys he had ever seen."[40]

Guggenheim Jeune's second season opened with *Exhibition of Paintings and Drawings by Children* (October 14–29), which included works by Peggy's daughter, Pegeen, and a teenage Lucian Freud. During this season, Piet Mondrian, then residing in London, visited the gallery and asked Peggy, much to her surprise and amusement, where the best nightclubs were, so that he could exercise his remarkable gift as a dancer. Peggy and the sculptor Llewellyn (the pseudonym by which she would refer to him in her memoirs) helped organize a three-day auction for a Spanish relief committee in November. From the auction, Peggy

herself bought her first Ernst painting and a Llewellyn for what she called "normal prices."[41] Her comment is indicative of the fact that, despite her generosity, she was invariably thrifty.

The second season continued with *Exhibition of Collages, Papiers-collés, and Photo-montages* (November 4–26), which was installed by Penrose and included works by Arp, Ernst, Kurt Schwitters, Taeuber-Arp, and Laurence Vail, among many others. Simultaneous solo exhibitions of pottery by Jill Salaman and works in various mediums by Marie Vassilieff (December 2–23) were followed by a show devoted to Grace W. Pailthorpe, a psychiatrist and surgeon, and Reuben Mednikoff (January 10–31, 1939), both of whom explored the unconscious through automatic paintings and drawings. Solo exhibitions for Wolfgang Paalen (February 15–March 11), John Tunnard (March 16–April 8),

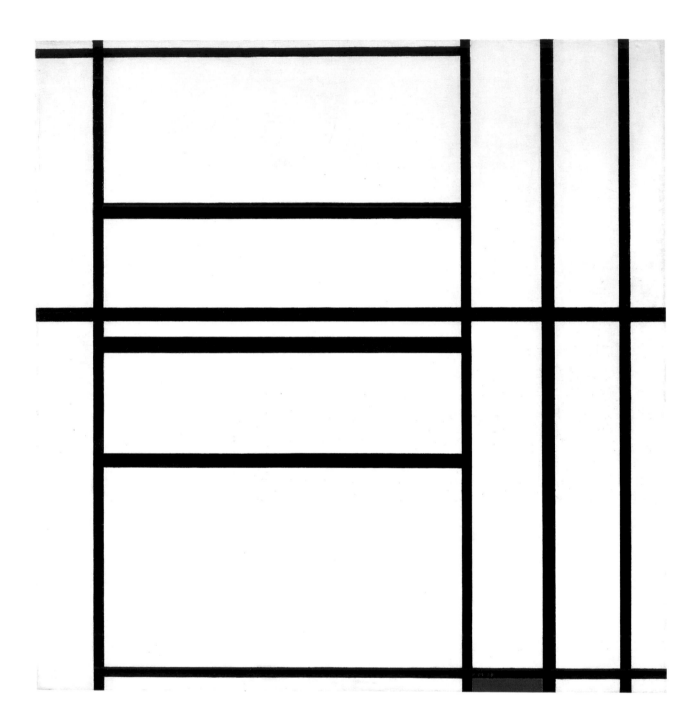

Henghes (April 14–May 6), and Charles Howard (April 14–May 6), led up to *Exhibition of Abstract and Concrete Art* (May 11–27), which included works by such artists as Arp, Calder, Barbara Hepworth, Kandinsky, Mondrian, and Ben Nicholson.[42]

Guggenheim Jeune closed after the simultaneous presentations of a solo exhibition for Julian Trevelyan (June 8–22) and *S. W. Hayter's Studio 17* (June 8–23). Read wrote the preface to the joint catalogue. At the urging of Llewellyn, two special series of signed prints from Stanley W. Hayter's Studio 17 were sold to benefit Spanish refugees. Peggy herself bought two sets: one illustrated Paul Eluard's poem "Solidarité," which had been translated into English by Beckett's friend the poet Brian Coffey; and the other illustrated Stephen Spender's poem "Fraternity," which had been translated into French by Louis Aragon. The prints were by such artists as Picasso, Kandinsky, Joan Miró, and Tanguy, among others. On June 22, a farewell party was held at Guggenheim Jeune during which the photographer Gisèle Freund showed "projections of colour-photography of famous contemporary artists."[43] Around this time, Freund photographed Peggy—wearing a classic string of pearls and bright red lipstick and nails that matched perfectly with the silk ribbon contour of her suit—together with Read, the two sitting earnestly in front of Tanguy's *The Sun in Its Jewel Case* (1937), which she had recently acquired.

Just a few months before, in March, Peggy had conceived the idea of opening a museum of Modern art because the gallery was losing money, despite its being a successful artistic and cultural venture. She approached Read, who had been the editor of *The Burlington Magazine* in London since 1933. In such books as *The Meaning of Art* (1931), *Art Now* (1933), *Art and Industry* (1934), *Art and Society* (1936), and *Surrealism* (1936), he wrote about art in general as well as contemporary art. He had been involved in organizing the 1936 *International Surrealist Exhibition*, and his friends included the circle of artists around Hepworth, Moore, and Nicholson. Through his writings and his active involvement with artists, he had done much to popularize avant-garde art in the English-speaking world. He had been interested in founding a museum of Modern art in Edinburgh, where he was teaching in 1931, but when he heard from Peggy that she wanted him to run a museum she was planning to create in London, he was skeptical at first. Penrose had been initially involved, but he and Peggy soon disagreed

FACING PAGE

Piet Mondrian
Composition, 1938–39
Oil on canvas, mounted on wood support; canvas 105.2 x 102.3 cm; wood support 109.1 x 106 x 2.5 cm
Peggy Guggenheim Collection
76.2553 PG 39

39

bitterly. Reluctant to renounce his secure post at *The Burlington Magazine,* Read finally decided to accept Peggy's offer as long as he could borrow one year's salary to buy a partnership in the publishing house Routledge. In return, he was ready to defer the first six months of his salary until the museum would open. Peggy cut back significantly on her personal expenses, as she believed that "every penny that I could raise was to be used for the museum."[44]

Peggy's proposed museum in London was modeled on the Museum of Modern Art in New York, whose departments and programs dealt not only with the traditional mediums of painting and sculpture but also with photography, design, film, and architecture. The London museum was intended to be a center for visual and performing arts, what Read referred to as "a sympathetic linking of all the arts in their modern aspects."[45] Proposals for a theater—for performances of music and recitals of poetry—a library, and various galleries were articulated. Read wrote:

> It is quite conceivable that, as it *may* develop, paintings will play only a subordinate part in the scheme. The idea is rather to create a focus for whatever creative activity and critical appreciation there is to be found in this country; to define and defend the modern tradition; to create an atmosphere in which that tradition can develop. . . . it will be a historic sequence in which each picture is a necessary link,

and historical significance will be even more important than aesthetic significance.[46]

Finding a suitable site was not easy, but then the London residence of art historian Kenneth Clark on Portland Place became available. Peggy was relatively oblivious to the impending war with Germany; she would later write with her usual honesty: "Lady Clark . . . told me she was going to live in the country to please her children. I was so silly I did not realize that she was preparing for the fast approaching war, and I thought I was very lucky to acquire her house."[47] (Indeed, war was declared in September, and the lease was never signed.) A list for the museum's opening exhibition had been drawn up with Read's help, and after a summer holiday in the south of France, Peggy left for Paris to negotiate loans of artworks.

A Picture a Day

When World War II began, Peggy abandoned her plans for a London museum and decided not to go back to England. She began to use Read's list—which would be revised by Peggy's friend Nelly van Doesburg, the widow of Theo van Doesburg, and Marcel Duchamp—as the basis for assembling a private collection of abstract and Surrealist art. Peggy took this opportunity to visit such artists as Albert Gleizes, Vasily Kandinsky, and Yves Tanguy, whose painting *Promontory Palace* (1931) she was able to buy from Tanguy's soon-to-be ex-wife, Jeannette. Peggy "conceived a wonderful scheme of forming an artists' colony for the duration of the war," but shortly came to her senses: "As soon as I got back to Paris and met a few of the people we had thought of inviting, I realized what a hell life would have been."[48] Although she had to face the unpleasant task of dismissing Herbert Read, they were to remain friends and continued to correspond with and see each other in the years to come. In fact, Peggy considered Read to be a father-figure who "treated me the way Disraeli treated Queen Victoria"[49]; he would often sign his letters to her with an affectionate "Papa."

In addition to Duchamp and Nelly van Doesburg, Peggy was helped in her endeavor by Howard Putzel, who had initially corresponded with her from California on the occasion of the opening of Guggenheim Jeune. He was passionate about Modern art and subsequently sent some of his own Tanguys to her Tanguy exhibition. He had already been befriended by Duchamp,

Max Ernst, and Tanguy, and—eager to get to know them in person—in 1938 he closed his gallery in Los Angeles and moved to Paris. He ended up meeting Peggy at the home of Mary Reynolds, and he was delighted to help her assemble a collection.

In the winter of 1938–39, Putzel introduced Peggy to Ernst, who was then involved with the painter Leonora Carrington. Peggy described Ernst as having "a handsome beak-like nose resembling a bird's. He was exquisitely made."[50] Possibly in order to please Ernst, Peggy bought Carrington's fantastic and rather sensuous *The Horses of Lord Candlestick* (1939). This was Carrington's first sale, and Peggy eventually gave the painting to Sindbad.

That winter, Peggy also spent time with the American composer and critic Virgil Thomson, who was her fond admirer. She "thought it would be nice to marry Virgil to have a musical background, but I never got far with the project"[51] (a comment perhaps intended as an inside joke given the fact that Thomson was a homosexual). He composed a musical portrait of Peggy in the form of his Piano Sonata no. 4 (*Guggenheim Jeune*), a "relatively straightforward tonal piece."[52] Peggy did not find it "in the least resembling" although she had "posed quietly for several hours" for Thomson.[53]

Peggy's life during the war was extraordinary to say the least. From the time war was declared at the beginning of September until April 1940, when the Germans invaded Norway and Denmark, a "phony war" seemed to be taking place. Many in Western Europe had been lulled into a false sense of security, but even as the Germans advanced through the Low Countries and on into France during May and June, Peggy remained undaunted by the situation. During this short period, Peggy assiduously bought works of art with the funds that had previously been allocated for her museum project. Her motto was "buy a picture a day."[54]

Peggy rented Kay Sage's apartment on the Ile Saint-Louis behind Nôtre-Dame on the quai d'Orléans. An American heiress and a painter, Sage—whom Peggy liked to call "Princess" because she was still married to an Italian prince—soon became Tanguy's wife. Peggy gave dinner parties in the apartment, which had a terrace and a big studio with plenty of light; she would remember being "happy as all my life I had wanted to live by a river."[55] It was a perfect time for Peggy, and she went to artists' studios and art dealers in order to buy artworks. The uncertainty of war

Antoine Pevsner and Peggy Guggenheim, 1940, with Pevsner's *Developable Surface* (*Surface développable*, 1938–August 1939), which she had recently purchased from him. Private collection

FACING PAGE

Constantin Brancusi
Bird in Space (*L'Oiseau dans l'espace*), 1932–40
Polished brass, 151.7 cm high, including base
Peggy Guggenheim Collection
76.2553 PG 51

meant that although artists were more anxious to sell, there were fewer buyers; artworks were more readily available, and the prices were quite cheap. A photograph by Rogi André, a former pupil and the first wife of André Kertész, shows a proud Peggy next to Constantin Brancusi's sculpture *Maiastra* (1912 [?]), which she bought from Nicole Groult, a sister of Paul Poiret. Peggy had previously failed to buy *Bird in Space* (1932–40) from Brancusi; she had an argument with the artist because she felt that he had demanded an excessively high price. Months later, Peggy succeeded in buying it at a discount with the help of van Doesburg and a good exchange rate.

Peggy bought a Jean Hélion painting (which she subsequently exchanged), little knowing he would later become her son-in-law. She purchased Salvador Dalí's *Birth of Liquid Desires* (1931–32) directly from his wife, Gala; although she did not particularly care for the Spanish painter, his name was on her list, and she was disciplined enough to buy his work. The acquisition of Alberto Giacometti's sculpture *Woman with Her Throat Cut* (1932, cast 1940) followed after Peggy went to visit the sculptor in his studio on avenue du Maine; he personally delivered it to the Ile Saint-Louis apartment. However, she had no luck with Pablo Picasso, who mistook her for a bourgeois housewife with her shopping list and dismissed her abruptly from his studio.

André's photographs of a lively and carefree Peggy seem all the more ironic as she shows off her latest acquisitions. During

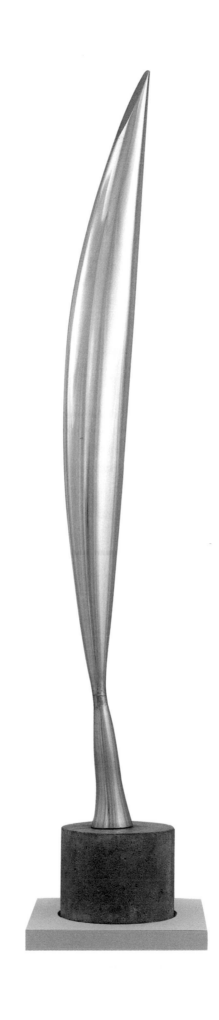

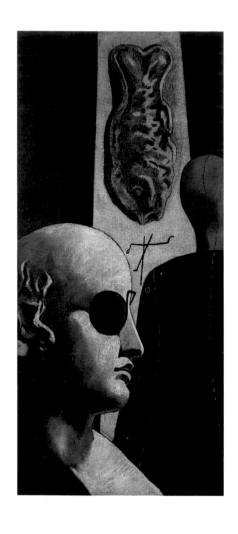

the last months before Paris fell to the Germans in June,
Peggy kept up the pace of her purchases, acquiring "fifty works,
thirty-seven of which are still in the collection"[56]: four Jean
Arps, one Giacomo Balla, two Brancusis, one Georges Braque,
one Giorgio de Chirico, two Dalís, one Robert Delaunay, one
Theo van Doesburg, one Raymond Duchamp-Villon, two Ernsts,
two Giacomettis, one Gleizes, one Paul Klee, one Fernand
Léger, one El Lissitzky, one René Magritte, three Man Rays,
one Louis Marcoussis, one Joan Miró, one Piet Mondrian, two
Pevsners, one Francis Picabia, one Kurt Schwitters, one Gino
Severini, one Georges Vantongerloo, and one Jacques Villon.
According to art historian Angelica Zander Rudenstine, "At least
twenty of those works were purchased directly from the individual artists, nine from dealers, four from Nelly van Doesburg . . .
and two from Duchamp. . . . Other works bought during
this same period were later given away or (in rare cases) sold."[57]

Peggy presently needed more space to store her growing
collection. After a failed attempt to secure the apartment where
Frédéric Chopin had died, on the place Vendôme, the most sensi-
ble thing seemed to be that the artworks should be sent out
of Paris. Léger suggested that the Musée du Louvre might give
her storage space in the country, where the museum was sending its own paintings, but she was told that hers "were too
modern and not worth saving."[58] After temporarily sending her
collection to a château outside Vichy—and with the Germans
advancing fast on Paris—Peggy finally decided to head to
the Alps to be near Laurence and their children, Pegeen and

ABOVE AND FACING PAGE, RIGHT

Peggy Guggenheim in Kay Sage's
apartment on the Ile Saint-Louis,
photographed around 1940 by Rogi André.
Bibliothèque Nationale de France, Paris,
Département des Estampes et de la
Photographie

FACING PAGE, LEFT

Giorgio de Chirico
The Nostalgia of the Poet
(*La Nostalgie du poète*), 1914
Oil and charcoal on canvas,
89.7 x 40.7 cm
Peggy Guggenheim Collection
76.2553 PG 65

Robert Delaunay
*Windows Open Simultaneously
1st Part, 3rd Motif (Fenêtres ouvertes
simultanément 1ère partie, 3e motif)*, 1912
Oil on canvas, 57 x 123 cm
Peggy Guggenheim Collection
76.2553 PG 36

Sindbad, who were living in Mégève. Peggy soon settled nearby in Grenoble, and luckily, Nelly van Doesburg was a friend of André Farcy, director of the Musée de Grenoble, who agreed to hide her artworks in the museum's cellar until they could be shipped to New York. Thanks to the good sense of Peggy's shipper, René Lefebvre-Foinet, the collection was packed among personal belongings, so that there would be less potential for problems with customs officials.

Passage to America

The situation for refugees—including artists, intellectuals, and political activists—in France was difficult and perilous. The Emergency Rescue Committee—formed under the auspices of the American Federation of Labor, the Museum of Modern Art, New York, and other groups—was run by an American, Varian Fry, who had come to France to provide refugees with passports and visas to the United States. Among the refugees were many Surrealists and their families. When not at their headquarters in Marseilles, Fry and his staff stayed nearby in a derelict villa called Air-Bel. André Breton and his family as well as the writer Victor Serge were also put up at the villa. Kay Sage cabled Peggy in Grenoble asking her to help finance the passage to America of the Bretons, Max Ernst, and Pierre Mabille, a favorite doctor of the Surrealists. After some protest, Peggy agreed to help the Bretons and Max. She also took up the cause of the Jewish Romanian artist Victor Brauner, but the Romanian quota was so small that he was unable to get a visa. She would continue to give financial support to Breton after he arrived in New York. Forever grateful for her help and generosity, he would write to her in 1965: "Je n'ai pas pour autant oublié New York, ni ce Marseille au tournant de 1940 d'où j'ai pu m'évader à temps grâce à vous. C'est évidemment une des grandes dates de ma vie et je ne pense jamais sans émotion que tout a dépendu alors de votre généreuse intervention."[59] (I have certainly not forgotten New York, nor Marseilles at the turn of 1940 when I was able to escape thanks to you. It is of course one of the important dates in my life and I never think without emotion that everything depended on your generous intervention.)

Peggy wrote to Max, at the suggestion of Laurence and René Lefebvre-Foinet, asking him for a painting in exchange for paying for his passage to America. She sent him money so that he could rescue some of his sculptures, which had been left in a house that Leonora Carrington had foolishly signed over to a Frenchman just before she left France. Peggy subsequently began an affair with Max, even though he was still pining after Carrington and was interested in Leonor Fini, whose painting *The Shepherdess of the Sphinxes* (1941) Peggy rather reluctantly bought at Max's instigation. By the spring of 1941, Max, Peggy, Laurence, and Kay Boyle were all waiting in Marseilles for passage to America. Laurence and Boyle were there with their own as well as Peggy's children; the couple's marriage was effectively over although they would not be legally divorced until 1943. This cast of characters moved on to Lisbon, where they awaited permission to leave for New York. Their life in a Lisbon hotel was a tragicomedy that confused and unsettled everyone's lives. Long meals, days at the beach, and excursions ensued.

Finally, on July 13, after an agonizing wait for a variety of legal papers, "eleven people: one husband, two ex-wives, one future husband and seven children"[60] boarded the Pan American Clipper in Lisbon to fly across the Atlantic to safer shores. After a long flight, Peggy, wearing a gigantic hat bought during a stop in the Azores, and entourage arrived in New York. Max's son, Jimmy Ernst, was there to meet them. He would write, movingly depicting Peggy as she came toward him, that "her body and walk suggest[ed] considerable hesitation. . . . Her face was strangely childlike, but it expressed something I imagined the ugly duckling must have felt the first time it saw its reflection in the water. . . . The anxiety-ridden eyes were warm and almost

Jacqueline and Aube Breton, Peggy Guggenheim, and André Breton at Villa Air-Bel, 1941.
Private collection, Courtesy of Aube Breton Elléouët

pleading, and the bony hands, at a loss where to go. . . . There was something about her that wanted me to reach out to her, even before she spoke."[61] Howard Putzel, "who resembled a well-worn teddy bear,"[62] had already returned to New York and was also there to greet them. He reassured Peggy that her collection had arrived safely. Max was detained for several days, pending a hearing, because he was traveling with a German passport although he had lived in France since 1922. Julien Levy, who was Max's dealer and Mina Loy's son-in-law, was ready to testify on Max's behalf as were trustees of the Museum of Modern Art, but he was soon released to Jimmy's custody. Jimmy, who got along well with Peggy, was already apprehensive about the relationship between her and his father.

Peggy and Max went to see her uncle Solomon's museum, the Museum of Non-Objective Painting, located in a former automobile showroom on East Fifty-fourth Street. She felt that "it really was a joke. There were about a hundred paintings by [Rudolf] Bauer . . . which overshadowed the twenty Kandinskys. . . . The museum was a beautiful little building completely wasted in this atrocious manner. Max called it the Bauer House; the Museum of Modern Art he called the Barr House [after its director, Alfred H. Barr, Jr.]; and [Albert E.] Gallatin's collection in the New York University building was the Bore House."[63] She also took him to visit Solomon's personal collection, which was housed in his apartment at the Plaza Hotel; in contrast, she called it "a really fine collection of modern paintings."[64] Max's favorite New York museum was the American Museum of Natural History, and he also loved the Museum of the American Indian, Heye Foundation.

Peggy and Max, accompanied by Pegeen and Jimmy, flew to San Francisco and then on to Los Angeles to visit her sister Hazel. Peggy was eager to see Louise and Walter Arensberg's superb collection at their Los Angeles home; among many other Modern masterpieces, the Arensbergs owned most of Marcel Duchamp's works (they later donated their collection to the Philadelphia Museum of Art). Peggy had already decided to revive her idea of establishing a museum and briefly looked for a site in California. However, she, Max, and the children soon departed by automobile to take a southern route back to New York. Traveling through Arizona, Max was transfixed by the desert landscapes he saw before him; they looked so much like the Surrealist landscapes he had painted from his imagination years ago in Europe.

By late September, Peggy and Max were back in New York, where they were destined to live in Hale House, a town house at 440 East Fifty-first Street and Beekman Place, overlooking the East River. Peggy believed that it was "the ideal place for the museum, except that it was too far away from the center of town. But we couldn't resist it. We intended to sleep in the servant's rooms when we were there, and to live in the country. However, we were not allowed to open a museum in this section. We had to take the house for ourselves to live in instead. It was the most beautiful house in New York."[65] It also had enough space for a studio for Max. Peggy's collection was casually displayed, mostly propped up against the walls, and the American Indian objects that Max had begun to collect during their trip across the Southwest were arranged throughout the house.

The Guggenheim-Ernst home quickly became a meeting place for displaced Surrealists and other European artists. Fantastic and memorable parties were held there, and it soon became one of the major social venues in the New York art world. Breton, happy to regroup his Surrealist colleagues and friends, was especially pleased to have reestablished friendly relations with Max, who had sided with Paul Eluard after a split among the Surrealists in 1938.

Peggy soon came to know Barr, James Thrall Soby, who would become Barr's successor as director of the Museum of Modern Art, and James Johnson Sweeney, later Rebay's successor as director of the Museum of Non-Objective Painting. Max sold many paintings and bought primitive art. Handsome and photogenic, he enjoyed being a celebrity in New York. He disliked being photographed with Peggy, however, although snapshots exist of them together with their dog Kachina, a Lhasa apso and the first of a long line of dogs that would keep Peggy company for the rest of her life.

On December 7, 1941, the United States entered World War II after the Japanese attacked the naval base at Pearl Harbor. Peggy—who had long been pressuring Max into marrying her—was especially distressed by "the idea of living in sin with an enemy alien."[66] With the United States now at war with the Axis powers—Germany, Italy, and Japan—she was eager to legalize their relationship, and they were married in a simple ceremony on December 30. Their new legal status did nothing to stop the awful fights they often had. Nor did it prevent Max from refusing to use the intimate form of address, *tu*, when addressing Peggy. Nor did it prevent him from seeing Leonora Carrington, who had also taken refuge in New York. He married Peggy but did not love her. Their marital incompatibility, however, did not slow down their social life. Parties continued unabated at Hale House, "the coolest place in New York,"[67] or at the home of their collector friends Bernard and Becky Reis.

Max had not yet included Peggy in any of his paintings. Then, one day in 1941, she noticed a small painting on his easel with several strange figures, one of which—with a horse's head— she read as being herself. Peggy called this painting *The Mystic Marriage* ("*The Antipope*," ca. 1941) and requested it as a wedding gift from him. He painted a larger version, entitled *The Antipope* (December 1941–March 1942), and the smaller one was thereafter given the same title (both are still in the Peggy Guggenheim Collection). Readings of Surrealist compositions are problematic, but it is valid to take into account the complex relationships that existed among Carrington, who was herself passionately interested in horses, Max, Pegeen, and Peggy when looking at the figures in the two paintings: "It is against this background of intense and entangled relationships that Ernst produced both versions."[68]

Breton and Max helped Peggy in the process of completing her collection, for which she decided to publish a catalogue. The book, more an anthology than a catalogue, was entitled *Art of This Century*. Ernst designed its cover, and Breton, who wrote a preface, encouraged her to include a selection of manifestos of artistic movements as well as artists' statements; photographs cropped to show only the artists' eyes were also included. Piet

Mondrian wrote a preface, which the painter Charmion von Wiegand translated into English. Dedicated to John Holms, the book was published in May 1942. Thirty works still in the Peggy Guggenheim Collection were purchased in New York during the few months before the publication of the catalogue; these include such paintings as Marc Chagall's *Rain* (1911), Duchamp's *Nude (Study), Sad Young Man on a Train* (1911–12), Vasily Kandinsky's *White Cross* (January–June 1922), and Joan Miró's *Seated Woman II* (February 27, 1939).[69]

Even before the influx of Surrealist refugees during World War II, there had been significant exposure to Surrealism in the United States. The first Surrealist exhibition in America, *Newer Super-Realism*, was held at the Wadsworth Atheneum in Hartford in 1931. Levy, who had been showing Surrealist art in his New York gallery since 1932, published an anthology, *Surrealism*, in 1936, and Barr organized the successful exhibition *Fantastic Art, Dada and Surrealism* at the Museum of Modern Art in the same year. In 1940, the Surrealist magazine *View* was founded by the poet Charles Henri Ford, who edited it until its final issue in 1947; Ford dedicated several issues to individual artists, such as Duchamp and Max Ernst. From November 1941 to January 1942, the Museum of Modern Art held simultaneous exhibitions of works by Salvador Dalí and Joan Miró.

In 1942, the exhibition *Artists in Exile*, which included both Surrealist and abstract artists, was held at Pierre Matisse's gallery in New York. In this year, Peggy was one of the sponsors of *Masters of Abstract Art*, an exhibition held at Helena Rubinstein's New Art Center on Fifth Avenue to benefit the American Red Cross. Rubinstein and Elsa Schiaparelli, yet another wartime resident, played important roles in the diffusion and understanding of Modern and contemporary art in New York during the war years. Peggy, Rubinstein, and Schiaparelli were, as the art historian Leo Steinberg has so rightly said, literally "living feminism."[70]

The art critic Clement Greenberg thought "the Surrealist influence has become exaggerated" and that before the war Americans had seen "more good contemporary art in New York: Miró, Matisse, Klee, Kandinsky. . . . We saw a lot more than the French did."[71] Greenberg believed that those masters of Modern European art had more of an influence on American art than any of the Surrealists. The presence of the émigrés, however, clearly had a tremendous impact on New York artists, and it

André Breton, Marcel Duchamp, and Max Ernst standing behind Morris Hirshfield's *Girl Looking Through a Doorway*, with Leonora Carrington seated, photographed at Peggy Guggenheim's East Fifty-first Street home around 1942–43 by Matta.
The Young-Mallin Archive, New York, A. Alpert Papers

was Matta (Roberto Sebastián Matta Echaurren) who probably had the most influence on the emerging Abstract Expressionists. A Chilean, he had been one of the younger members of the Surrealist circle in Paris. He organized evenings of Surrealist exercises, during which such artists as William Baziotes, Jackson Pollock, and Robert Motherwell became familiar with automatism. Matta—fluent in English and personable—belonged to the same generation as these Americans, and he was able to undercut the influence of Breton.

Art of This Century

In 1942, Peggy still trying to get her museum started, finally leased space on the top floor at 30 West Fifty-seventh Street. At Howard Putzel's recommendation, Peggy asked the avant-garde architect Frederick Kiesler to design the galleries. In her first letter to Kiesler, dated February 26, she wrote, "Will you give me some advise [sic] about remodelling two tailor-shops into an Art Gallery?"[72] He felt challenged by the project, submitting a proposal on March 7, in which he acknowledged, "It is your wish that some new method be developed for exhibiting paintings, drawings, sculptures, collages and so called: objects."[73] As the curator Lisa Phillips would later write, Kiesler was given a unique opportunity to test "unorthodox ideas about the presentation of art in a fantastic Surrealist environment that merged architecture, art, light, sound and motion."[74] He was intent on breaking down barriers between viewers and works of art. The displays were constructed to be "mobile and demountable," in Kiesler's words.[75] Most important, all the paintings were to be exhibited without their frames, free of yet another level of confinement. Kiesler wrote:

> Today, the framed painting on the wall has become a decora-
> tive cipher without life and meaning. . . . Its frame is at
> once symbol and agent of an artificial duality of "vision" and
> "reality," or "image" and "environment," a plastic barrier
> across which man looks from the world he inhabits to the
> alien world in which the work of art has its being. That
> barrier must be dissolved: the frame, today reduced to an
> arbitrary rigidity, must regain its architectural, spatial
> significance. The two opposing worlds must be seen again as
> jointly indispensable forces in the same world. The ancient
> magic must be recreated whereby the God and the mask of

the God, the deer and the image of the deer existed with equal potency, with the same immediate reality in one living universe.[76]

Kiesler had already begun to develop a method of spatial exhibition in Vienna in 1924, and Peggy's commission presented him with the perfect forum for fully bringing his ideas to fruition. Art of This Century, as the museum/gallery came to be called, contained four exhibition galleries, and a satisfied Peggy considered it "very theatrical and extremely original."[77] The abstract gallery "had movable walls made of stretched deep-blue canvas, laced to the floors and ceiling. . . . The floors were painted turquoise, Peggy's favorite color. Unframed pictures 'swaying in space' at eye level were actually mounted on triangular floor-to-ceiling rope pulleys resembling cat's cradles."[78]

The walls and ceiling of the Surrealist gallery were painted black. Unframed paintings were mounted on cantilevered wooden arms that protruded from the curved gumwood panels attached to the walls. Viewers were free to adjust the angles at which they viewed the paintings.

The kinetic gallery featured interactive displays. Works by Paul Klee were mounted on a mechanized belt that was set in motion by an electric eye. In order to see fourteen reproductions from Marcel Duchamp's *Box in a Valise* (1941), viewers had to peep through a hole and turn a wheel. A third kinetic object was a shadow box that displayed André Breton's *Portrait of the Actor A. B.* (1942); after lifting a lever, a diaphragm imprinted with Breton's image opened to reveal the poem-object within (the object was either destroyed or is lost).

The daylight gallery and painting library shared one space. This gallery, more conventionally designed with white painted walls, was used for temporary exhibitions, and the windows along Fifty-seventh Street were covered with transparent fabric to filter the daylight. Within the same space, visitors could sit on folding stools and study the library of paintings that were stored in and could be displayed on open bins specially designed by Kiesler.

Throughout Art of This Century were Kiesler's furniture units—in the form of biomorphic objects—that could be used for seating or for the display of artworks. Sculptures sat on some of the units, and paintings were mounted on sawed-off baseball bats that protruded from others. Kiesler believed that "no matter what the success of the enterprise—these galleries represent

Vasily Kandinsky
White Cross (Weisses Kreuz),
January–June 1922
Oil on canvas, 100.5 x 110.6 cm
Peggy Guggenheim Collection
76.2553 PG 34

Installation view of the abstract
gallery at Art of This Century,
photographed around 1942 by
Berenice Abbott.
Solomon R. Guggenheim Museum

the result of a splendid co-operation between the workmen, the
owner and the designer."[79]

Elsa Schiaparelli asked Peggy to help organize a Surrealist
exhibition to benefit the Coordinating Council of French Relief
Societies. Peggy sent her to Breton, who, with the help of
Max Ernst and Duchamp, organized *First Papers of Surrealism*,
which was held in the Whitelaw Reid mansion on Madison
Avenue. Duchamp decorated the interior with miles of string
forming a huge web; viewers could hardly see the art, but
the effect was stunning. Peggy headed the list of sponsors for the
exhibition, which opened on October 14. Less than a week later,
on the night of October 20, Art of This Century opened; one-dollar
entry tickets benefited the American Red Cross. The opening—
for which Peggy said she wore "one of my Tanguy earrings

and one made by [Alexander] Calder, in order to show my impartiality between Surrealist and abstract art"[80]—was a huge success with favorable articles appearing in the press.

Art of This Century came on the scene at a time, when, as Sidney Janis would recall, "there were maybe a dozen galleries in all of New York."[81] It became such a popular meeting place for casual visitors, as well as for European and American artists, that Peggy took the unusual step of charging an admission fee of twenty-five cents, which she herself often collected. Eventually, she gave in to criticism from Putzel, as well as from Bernard Reis and Laurence Vail, against the practice and reverted to free admission. Peggy left her troubles with Max at home in the morning and spent the day at the gallery greeting visitors and planning exhibitions. Her relations with Jimmy Ernst continued to be friendly—indeed far more pleasant than those with his father—and for a short time he worked as her assistant. Peggy had decided, on the advice of Reis, that Art of This Century should not only be a museum space that exhibited European masters but also a commercial gallery that sold the paintings of young American artists.

The temporary exhibitions held during the first season began with a triple presentation in December: *Objects by Joseph Cornell*; *Marcel Duchamp: Box-Valise*; and *Laurence Vail: Bottles*. Five of the Cornell objects exhibited, including *Fortune Telling Parrot (Parrot Music Box)* (ca. 1937–38), entered Peggy's collection. Duchamp's leather valise contained replicas of his works and included one original photographic reproduction. The collage bottles by Laurence—a "greatly gifted artist," according to Greenberg[82]—were pioneering examples of assemblage. Wine bottles turned into works of art, they are intimate, often humorous objects onto which he pasted scraps of newspaper and magazine pictures, tattered materials, found objects, and shells.

At Duchamp's instigation, Peggy held an exhibition wholly dedicated to women. *Exhibition by 31 Women* (January 5, 1942–February 6, 1943) was selected by a jury that consisted of Breton, Duchamp, Jimmy Ernst, Max Ernst, Putzel, James Thrall Soby, James Johnson Sweeney, and Peggy. Peggy had asked Max to visit the women's studios, and one of the artists he visited was Dorothea Tanning, then married to a naval officer. Peggy considered Tanning to be "pretentious, boring, stupid, vulgar and dressed in the worst possible taste but was quite talented and imitated Max's painting, which flattered him immensely"[83]; she always thought that Leonora Carrington

Peggy Guggenheim wearing earring with miniature painting by Yves Tanguy, 1949.
Private collection.
© Cameraphoto–Epoche, Venice

Joseph Cornell
Fortune Telling Parrot (Parrot Music Box),
ca. 1937–38
Box construction, 40.8 x 22.2 x 17 cm
Peggy Guggenheim Collection
76.2553 PG 126

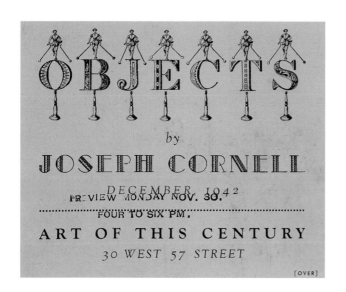

was superior to Tanning. Nonetheless, Max and Tanning began an affair, and they would marry in 1946 in a double ceremony with Man Ray and Juliet Browner. *Exhibition by 31 Women* included works by Xenia Cage (then married to John Cage), Leonora Carrington, Louise Nevelson, Meret Oppenheim, Irene Rice Pereira, Kay Sage, Hedda Sterne, Sophie Taeuber-Arp, Tanning, and Pegeen Vail, among others. Devastated by Max's involvement with Tanning, Peggy had to concede that her unhappy life with him was at an end. They separated and divorced soon afterward.

The opening for the next exhibition, *Retrospective Exhibition of the Works of Hélion* (February 8–March 13), was a benefit for Fighting French Relief. Jean Hélion first met Pegeen at this time, and they would marry in 1944. A group exhibition entitled *15 Early 15 Late Paintings* (March 13–April 17) was conceived by Jimmy Ernst; it paired an early and a late painting by fifteen European painters, such as Georges Braque, Salvador Dalí, Vasily Kandinsky, Fernand Léger, Joan Miró, and Piet Mondrian. At roughly the same time as her separation from Max and a rift with Breton, Peggy began to distance herself from the French Surrealists and increased her involvement with young American artists. In *Exhibition of Collage* (April 16–May 15), the first international exhibition of collage held in the United States, such established European artists as Braque, George Grosz, then living in New York, Pablo Picasso, and Kurt Schwitters were shown alongside such American artists as William Baziotes, Cornell, David Hare, Robert Motherwell, Pereira, Jackson Pollock (his name misspelled on the announce-

Exhibition announcement (recto) for *Objects by Joseph Cornell* and (verso) for *Marcel Duchamp: Box-Valise* and *Laurence Vail: Bottles*, 1942. Solomon R. Guggenheim Museum Archives, Bequest of Peggy Guggenheim, 1976

Laurence Vail
Untitled, 1941
Glass bottle and collage, 21 cm high
Peggy Guggenheim Collection
76.2553 PG 289

61

ment as "Polloch"), Ad Reinhardt, and Sterne; works by Jimmy Ernst and Laurence Vail were also included. Motherwell and Pollock were uneasy about collage but very much wanted to be in the exhibition; Motherwell remembers that Pollock "had no particular feel for collage, but I remember being surprised at the violence on his attack of the material."[84]

Pollock—who coincidentally was working as a custodian at the Museum of Non-Objective Painting—Baziotes, Jimmy Ernst, Motherwell, Pereira, Reinhardt, and Sterne also appeared in the subsequent *Spring Salon for Young Artists* (May 18–June 26), as did such artists as Morris Graves, Matta, and Gordon Onslow-Ford. This exhibition was a unique opportunity to see the newest American art; most New York galleries showed the work of European artists. The jury consisted of Barr, Duchamp, Mondrian, Putzel, Soby, Sweeney, and Peggy, with Breton and Max Ernst conspicuously absent. To Peggy's surprise, Mondrian was especially taken by the work of Pollock, whom he thought was the most exciting painter he had seen for a very long time. Reviews were good, and Greenberg wrote in *The Nation*, "there is a large painting [*Stenographic Figure*, 1942, now in the collection of the Museum of Modern Art, New York] by Jackson Pollock, which, I am told, made the jury starry-eyed."[85] At the urging of Matta and Putzel, Peggy took the unusual, almost unique, step of signing a contract with the young artist, under the terms of which he would receive a monthly stipend. The contract would be renewed annually, and Peggy continued to pay a stipend through February 1948.

Exhibition announcement for *Exhibition of Collage*, 1943, with (recto) detail of Laurence Vail's *Screen*, 1940, and (verso) incomplete listing of participating artists. Solomon R. Guggenheim Museum Archives, Bequest of Peggy Guggenheim, 1976

After opening the second season of Art of This Century by presenting the loan exhibition *Masterworks of Early de Chirico* (October 5–November 7), which was based on Soby's 1941 book *The Early de Chirico*, Peggy gave Pollock his first solo exhibition (November 9–27). The preface to Pollock's catalogue was written by Sweeney, and Peggy considered Pollock to be the "spiritual offspring" of Sweeney and herself.[86] Reviews by Robert Coates in *The New Yorker* and Clement Greenberg in *The Nation* were full of praise. In *Partisan Review*, Motherwell wrote that Pollock "represents one of the younger generation's chances. There are not three other young Americans of whom this could be said."[87] At the instigation of Sweeney, the Museum of Modern Art put a reserve on *She-Wolf* (1943), but Barr, who disliked Pollock's work, was resistant to purchasing it. A reproduction of the painting appeared in the April 1944 issue of *Harper's Bazaar*, accompanying an article by Sweeney entitled "Five American Painters," and in May the Museum of Modern Art finally approved the purchase, making it Pollock's first work to be acquired by a museum. Over the years, several of Pollock's paintings were sold, but never for more than a thousand dollars each. Peggy eventually gave away well over a dozen of his paintings, much to her later distress, not realizing how important he would become in the history of American and Western painting.

In her personal life, Peggy had found solace in the friendship of Kenneth Macpherson, a wealthy patron of the arts, who was then married to the poet Bryher (Winifred Ellerman). (Bryher had previously been married to Robert McAlmon, one of Peggy's early Paris friends, and was involved in an ongoing relationship with the poet H. D. [Hilda Doolittle].) Macpherson met Peggy through Max, and in the aftermath of the couple's separation, they became close friends. Agreeing to an unconventional domestic arrangement, Peggy and Macpherson moved into a duplex apartment in a brownstone at 155 East Sixty-first Street; in effect, they were able to have separate apartments on each floor.

Macpherson advised Peggy on how to dress and make herself up nicely, and gave her financial guidance. Peggy had never been conventionally elegant; the artist Nell Blaine would recall that she was like a "sexy witch."[88] Jean Connolly, who had been married to the writer Cyril Connolly and would marry Laurence Vail in 1946, stayed at the duplex, where she "often shared a bed with her hostess."[89] Clearly, although Macpherson was a calming presence, Peggy's personal life was not much less confused than during her prior relationships.

Pollock was commissioned to paint *Mural* (December 1943, now in the collection of the Museum of Art, University of Iowa, Iowa City), his largest work, for the duplex. In 1945, André Kertész, who admired Peggy, would photograph her in her sitting room with Paul Delvaux's *The Break of Day* (*L'Aurore*, July 1937) in the background, and her earrings hanging on the walls. The duplex, like Hale House before it, became an important gathering place for members of New York's cultural world.

The 1943–44 season at Art of This Century continued with *Natural, Insane, Surrealist Art* (December 1–31); "natural" referred to "driftwood, petrified tree roots, bones and skeletons,"[90] which were shown along with drawings by the insane and a selection of Surrealist works by European and American artists. The second season continued into 1944 with solo exhibitions devoted to Pereira (January 4–22), Jean Arp (January 24–February 29), and—at the suggestion of Pollock and Lee Krasner—the first solo exhibition of Hans Hofmann (March 7–31). Hélion, Morris Hirshfield, Matta, Motherwell, Pollock, and Mark Rothko were among the diverse artists represented in *First Exhibition in America of Twenty Paintings* (April 11–30). The second *Spring Salon for Young Artists* (May 2–June 3) was juried by Barr, Duchamp, Macpherson, Putzel, Soby, Sweeney, and Peggy; Baziotes, Jimmy Ernst, Hare, Pereira, Pollock, Richard Pousette-Dart, and Sterne were among those exhibiting works. The season closed with *The Negro in American Life* (May 29–June 3), a photographic exhibition organized by John Becker with the Council Against Intolerance in America. This exhibition was such a success that a book of the same title was published later that year.

The third season started off with a succession of solo exhibitions of works by Baziotes (October 3–21), Motherwell

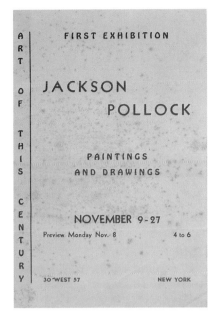

Exhibition announcement for *Jackson Pollock: Paintings and Drawings*, 1943. Solomon R. Guggenheim Museum Archives, Bequest of Peggy Guggenheim, 1976

(October 24–November 11), and Hare (November 14–December 2). These were Baziotes's and Hare's first solo exhibitions and Motherwell's first solo exhibition in the United States. Peggy had become friends with Jane and Paul Bowles, and in October she financed a recording of Paul Bowles's music under the label Art of This Century Recordings. The record cover was designed by Max Ernst, and only 100 copies were printed. The A-side was an early Sonata for Flute and Piano played by René Le Roy and George Reeves; the B-side was "Two Mexican Dances" played by the piano duo Arthur Gold and Robert Fizdale.

Barr and Sweeney were now her mentors; their roles in Peggy's life were roughly similar to the one previously played by Herbert Read. She also found Putzel, who had succeeded Jimmy Ernst as her assistant, to be indispensable in steering her to new discoveries. In fact, it was Putzel who proselytized for many of the artists—including the sculptor Hare and such then obscure painters as Baziotes, Hofmann, Pollock, Rothko, and Still—who were given their first solo exhibitions at Art of This Century. In the fall of 1944, Putzel—who had stopped working for Peggy after Hofmann's exhibition—opened his 67 Gallery, also on Fifty-seventh Street, where he exhibited contemporary American artists. The gallery's first season would be its last, as Putzel died of a heart attack during the summer of 1945.

The 1944–45 season at Art of This Century continued with simultaneous exhibitions of constructions by Isabelle Waldberg and paintings by Rudolph Ray (December 12–January 6). There followed solo exhibitions for the artists Mark Rothko (January 9–February 4), his first individual showing; Laurence Vail (February 10–March 16), again exhibiting collage bottles; Alberto Giacometti (February 10–March 16); Pollock (March 19–April 14); Wolfgang Paalen (April 17–May 12); and Alice Rahon Paalen (May 15–June 7). Pollock's second solo exhibition included open hours for viewing *Mural* at Peggy's duplex on Sixty-first Street. Greenberg wrote that the exhibition "establishes him, in my opinion, as the strongest painter of his generation and perhaps the greatest one to appear since Miró."[91] The season ended with *The Women* (June 12–July 7), the gallery's second group exhibition dedicated to women artists; it included many of the artists shown in 1943 as well as Louise Bourgeois and Janet Sobel—"the best woman painter by far in America," according to Peggy[92]—Sterne, and Charmion von Wiegand.

The fourth season at Art of This Century opened with *Autumn Salon* (October 6–29), which included many artists

FACING PAGE

Robert Motherwell
Personage (Autoportrait),
December 9, 1943
Paper collage, gouache, and ink on board,
103.8 x 65.9 cm
Peggy Guggenheim Collection
76.2553 PG 155

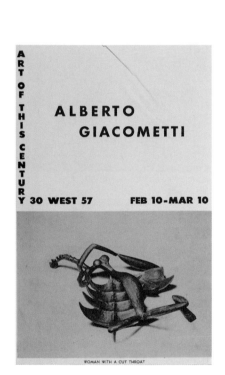

ART OF THIS CENTURY

ALBERTO
GIACOMETTI

30 WEST 57   FEB 10-MAR 10

WOMAN WITH A CUT THROAT

Exhibition announcement for *Alberto Giacometti*, 1945, with illustration of Giacometti's *Woman with Her Throat Cut* (*Femme égorgée*, 1932, cast 1940). Solomon R. Guggenheim Museum Archives, Bequest of Peggy Guggenheim, 1976

FACING PAGE

Peggy Guggenheim in her Sixty-first Street apartment, photographed in 1945 by André Kertész.
Estate of André Kertész

previously exhibited at the gallery as well as such newcomers as Willem de Kooning and Clyfford Still. Solo exhibitions by Charles Seliger (October 30–November 17), a friend of Jimmy Ernst; Paul Wilton (October 30–November 17); Lee Hersch (November 20–December 8); and Ted Bradley (November 20–December 8) were followed by *Christmas Exhibition of Gouaches* (December 11–29), which included a work by Arshile Gorky. Gorky's participation was surprisingly the only time he was shown at the gallery, although sometime around 1945 Peggy bought one of his mature paintings, *Untitled* (summer 1944), for her collection. The remainder of the season was devoted to solo exhibitions: Sobel (January 3–19, 1946), Hare (January 22–February 9), Still (February 12–March 7), Pamela Bodin (February 12–March 7), Pegeen Vail (March 9–30), Peter Busa (March 9–30), Pollock (April 2–20), Teresa Zarnower (April 23–May 11), Robert De Niro (April 23–May 11), and Sonja Sekula (May 14–June 1). Still's exhibition, his first individual showing, had been proposed by Rothko, who wrote the catalogue preface, and installed by Greenberg and David Porter. Peggy occasionally bought works that were in the exhibitions, and she purchased Still's *Jamais* (May 1944). He would later write, "Peggy was the only one doing an honest job at this time. She was doing something personal. The closing of her gallery [after the 1946–47 season] was the biggest loss to the art world."[93] De Niro (the father of the actor Robert De Niro) was praised by Greenberg for the abstractions in his first solo exhibition. Reviewing Pollock's third solo exhibition, Greenberg wrote that the artist's "superiority to his contemporaries in this country lies in his ability to create a genuinely violent and extravagant art without losing stylistic control."[94]

In March, the publication of Peggy's memoirs *Out of This Century: The Informal Memoirs of Peggy Guggenheim*—the title a play on the gallery's name—coincided with Pegeen's first solo exhibition. Max Ernst had provided art for the front of the dust jacket, and Pollock had done so for the back. In discussing certain relationships, Peggy amusingly used fictitious names, for example, "Florenz Dale" for Laurence Vail and "Oblomov" for Samuel Beckett. She spared no details in discussing her sexual affairs or the treatment she received during her marriage to Max, whom she referred to by name. The book received many reviews, mostly harsh, by such critics as Katharine Kuh, who called the memoirs a "vulgar autobiography" that was "doubly offensive" because of Peggy's "discriminating collection."[95]

Herbert Read, however, upon receiving a copy from Peggy, promptly wrote to her:

> You have probably concluded that I am "mortally offended" by the book, + am never going to speak to you again. Not a bit! . . . You have outrivalled Rousseau + Casanova, so who am I to criticize "Out of this Century"? I found it quite fascinating as an historical document—and it is only the lack of introspection + self-analysis which prevents it from being a human, psychological document (masterpiece?) like "Nightwood." That is why it is nearer to Casanova than to Rousseau—you are destined to be called the Female Casanova! It is perhaps even more amoral than even Casanova, who, if my memory is not deceiving me, has some snivelling moments of self-disgust, or self-pity.[96]

Writing in a rather matter-of-fact fashion, like a reporter just telling the facts, Peggy showed enthusiasm, without being really passionate. She did not want or was unable to completely reveal herself, being perhaps too emotionally vulnerable. In 1960, an edition—*Confessions of an Art Addict*—was published for which Peggy condensed her original memoirs, added new material, and used all real names except for "Llewellyn." In a letter to Peggy, Djuna Barnes wrote: "For myself I find it somewhat changed from the first as you are somewhat changed from those days. Just what was your purpose in re-writing it?"[97] In 1979, Peggy herself wrote in the third, final version—*Out of This Century: Confessions of an Art Addict*—"I seem to have written the first book as an uninhibited woman and the second one as a lady who was trying to establish her place in the history of modern art."[98]

World War II ended in Europe in May 1945 and in Asia that August. With the war over, Peggy decided she badly wanted to go back to Europe. Much as she loved Art of This Century, she loved Europe more. By the summer of 1946, Peggy, having decided against living in London, went first to Paris, where Sindbad and Pegeen had settled. There, Peggy ran into the writer Mary McCarthy, an old friend, and her husband, Bowden Broadwater, who were on their way to Venice. They encouraged Peggy to accompany them, and she was glad to leave Paris, where she now felt like a stranger. She would write:

> On my way there, I decided Venice would be my future home. I had always loved it more than any place on earth and felt

I would be happy alone there. I set about trying to find a palace that would house my collection and provide a garden for my dogs. This was to take several years; in the meantime I had to go back to New York to close the gallery.[99]

McCarthy's time with Peggy in Italy is vividly related in her story "The Cicerone," in which Peggy is fictionalized as "Polly Herkimer Grabbe," who is looking for a palazzo in Venice and to whom "men were a continental commodity of which one naturally took advantage, along with the wine and the olives, the bitter coffee and the crusty bread."[100]

Back in New York, Peggy made it clear that Art of This Century's 1946–47 season would be its last. The only group exhibition of this fifth and final season presented work by Seliger, Kenneth Scott (later a fashion designer), Dwight Ripley, John Goodwin, and David Hill (December 3–21). Otherwise the season consisted entirely of solo exhibitions: Hans Richter (October 22–November 9); Rudi Blesh (November 12–30); Virginia Admiral (November 12–30); Marjorie McKee (December 24–January 11); Helen Schwinger (December 24–January 11); Pollock (January 14–February 7); Hirshfield (February 1–March 1), a memorial exhibition of his last paintings; Pousette-Dart (March 4–22); Hare (March 25–April 19); and Theo van Doesburg (April 29–May 31), his first American retrospective.

Richter's exhibition consisted of an "orchestration of organic and inorganic forms,"[101] which included stills for his color film *Dreams That Money Can Buy* (1947). Under the auspices of Art

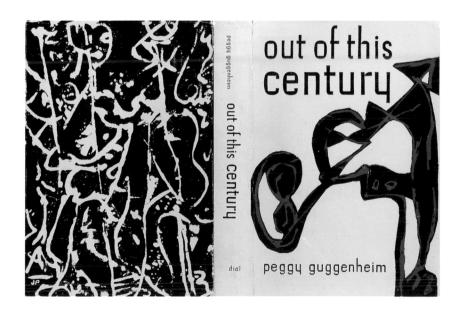

Dust jacket of Peggy Guggenheim's *Out of This Century: The Informal Memoirs of Peggy Guggenheim*, 1946, with front cover by Max Ernst and back cover by Jackson Pollock.
Private collection

Lee Krasner and Jackson Pollock,
photographed in the late 1940s by Wilfrid
Zogbaum.
Private collection

FACING PAGE

Jackson Pollock
Enchanted Forest, 1947
Oil on canvas, 221.3 x 114.6 cm
Peggy Guggenheim Collection
76.2553 PG 151

of This Century Productions, Peggy provided most of the financing for the film although only Macpherson's name appears in the credits as coproducer. Probably the first feature-length avant-garde film produced in America, it contained seven dream sequences on which Ernst, Léger, Man Ray, Duchamp, Calder (two dreams), and Richter collaborated; Paul Bowles, John Cage, and Darius Milhaud were among the composers contributing to the score.

Pollock's fourth solo exhibition again confirmed Peggy's prescience in giving financial support to the artist. Pollock exhibited paintings from two series, *Sounds in the Grass* and *Accabonac Creek*, and Greenberg thought the exhibition "signals what may be a major step in his development. . . . Pollock has gone beyond the stage where he needs to make his poetry explicit in ideographs. What he invents instead has perhaps, in its very abstractness and absence of assignable definition, a more reverberating meaning. . . . Pollock points a way beyond the easel."[102] Nonetheless, Pollock's work did not sell well, and few dealers were ready to represent him. Peggy finally succeeded in placing Pollock with Betty Parsons, who would first exhibit his work at her gallery in January 1948; Peggy herself paid Pollock the stipend due under his contract through February. After the van Doesburg exhibition, which had been arranged by Nelly van Doesburg, Peggy closed and completely dismantled the gallery. She sold Kiesler's furniture to the Museum of Modern Art and individually to people who dropped by, such as Sidney Janis. Seliger sold Kiesler's curved walls to the Franklin Simon department store, where he was working at the time. Peggy was eager to return to Italy.

In his review of the van Doesburg exhibition in *The Nation,* Greenberg honored Peggy:

> Her departure is in my opinion a serious loss to living American art. The erratic gaiety with which Miss Guggenheim promoted "non-realistic" art may have misled some people, as perhaps her autobiography did too, but the fact remains that in the three or four years of her career as a New York gallery director she gave first showings to more serious new artists than anyone else in the country. . . . I am convinced that Peggy Guggenheim's place in the history of American art will grow larger as time passes and as the artists she encouraged mature.[103]

The 1948 Biennale

During the summer of 1947, Peggy went to Venice and found
temporary quarters in the hotel Savoia e Jolanda on the Riva
degli Schiavoni. She set about exploring and rediscovering
La Serenissima (literally meaning "the most serene," this was an
historic name for the Republic of Venice). Thanks to the propri-
etor of the Café Angelo near the Rialto bridge, she went to the
restaurant All'Angelo just off the piazza San Marco in search of
the artist Emilio Vedova. All'Angelo was known as "il ritrovo
degli artisti" (the artists' hangout), and here she met Vedova and
Giuseppe Santomaso, both of whom had heard of Peggy as well
as of her uncle Solomon's Museum of Non-Objective Painting in
New York. In a mixture of English, French, and Italian, Peggy
spoke to the two abstract artists—both founding members of the
Fronte Nuovo delle Arti—spending many happy hours convers-
ing about art and her future in Venice. Santomaso was particularly interested in the problems of rendering color and light—
suggested by the mosaics of the neighborhood of San Marco and
the island of Torcello, and by the lagoon, canals, and familiar
sites of his native Venice.

In November, Peggy accompanied Jean Connolly and
Laurence Vail to Capri. By spring 1948, she was back in Venice,
where she rented an apartment in the Palazzo Barbaro, across
from the Accademia on the Grand Canal; Henry James had lived
in this palazzo during the writing of *The Wings of the Dove*
(1902). Because she had not yet found a permanent home for
either herself (and her dogs) or her collection, Santomaso suggested to Rodolfo Pallucchini, secretary-general of the Venice

Biennale, that Peggy's collection should be exhibited. Greece was embroiled in civil war, and the Greek government agreed that its pavilion—which would otherwise have been vacant—could be used to exhibit Peggy's collection. The pavilion was soon handsomely refurbished by the architect Carlo Scarpa. Although the *Biennale* had been founded in 1895, it was really not until 1948, the year of the first *Biennale* since 1942, that Venice began to play an international role in Modern and contemporary art. The 1948 *Biennale* (June 6–September 30) featured a prestigious presentation of Impressionist paintings curated by the art historian Roberto Longhi and a retrospective of Pablo Picasso paintings from 1907 to 1942. Restitution of a kind was made by the exhibition in the central pavilion of works by Otto Dix, Karl Hofer, and Max Pechstein, whose art had been labeled "degenerate" by the Nazis. Among the foreign pavilions, the American exhibition of a diverse group of seventy-nine artists, each represented by

Peggy Guggenheim in the pavilion *Collezione Peggy Guggenheim* at the Venice *Biennale*, photographed in June 1948 by Lee Miller for Condé Nast Publications.
Solomon R. Guggenheim Museum Archives, Bequest of Peggy Guggenheim, 1976.
© Lee Miller Archives

LEFT

Peggy Guggenheim and Lionello Venturi in the pavilion *Collezione Peggy Guggenheim* at the Venice *Biennale*, photographed in June 1948 by Lee Miller for Condé Nast Publications.
Solomon R. Guggenheim Museum Archives, Bequest of Peggy Guggenheim, 1976.
© Lee Miller Archives

a single work, included Stuart Davis, Arthur Dove, Marsden Hartley, John Marin, Georgia O'Keeffe, Maurice Prendergast, and Max Weber.

Collezione Peggy Guggenheim was a defining event of the *Biennale*. Peggy's collection was the most comprehensive survey of abstract and Surrealist art yet seen in Italy, and such American artists as William Baziotes, Jackson Pollock, Mark Rothko, and Clyfford Still were for the first time being shown outside the United States. Peggy's collection gave Europeans the opportunity to catch up with the best avant-garde art of the recent past and to be introduced to the New York painters who would come to dominate the art scene of the 1950s. Although Peggy's collection was featured in the *Biennale*'s catalogue, she also published a small catalogue to sell in the pavilion.

Peggy would later write, "My exhibition had enormous publicity and the pavilion was one of the most popular of the Biennale. . . . what I enjoyed most was seeing the name Guggenheim appearing on the maps in the Public Gardens next to the names of Great Britain, France, Holland. . . . I felt as though I were a new European country."[104] Peggy was honored with visits from Luigi Einaudi, the president of Italy, and James Dunn, the American ambassador to Italy. Another distinguished visitor was the elderly art historian Bernard Berenson, who disliked Modern art (perhaps his visit was suggested by Peggy's friend Elsa Schiaparelli, who was his son's mother-in-law). A defensive Peggy, who had read and admired Berenson's books, told him, "I couldn't afford old masters, and anyhow I consider it one's duty to protect the art of one's time."[105] To which Berenson retorted, "You should have come to me, my dear, I would have found you bargains."[106] Significantly, he liked Pollock's paintings, which "to him, were like tapestries."[107] A photograph by Lee Miller charmingly captured an ecstatic Peggy being visited in her pavilion by art critic Lionello Venturi. In British *Vogue*, Miller described Peggy's pavilion as the "most sensational" of all.[108] Peggy's *Biennale* experience was marred by a few incidents: a small sculpture by David Hare was stolen, and Pallucchini decided to remove a drawing by Matta, which he found too sexually explicit. And the intense publicity generated by her participation in the *Biennale* resulted in her being incessantly pursued: "I was plagued by everyone wanting to sell me something."[109] She hired Vittorio Carrain, one of the owners of All'Angelo, to assist her, and he became her part-time secretary.

The 1948 *Biennale* was a boost to the cultural life of Venice, and to Italy in general. During the next twenty years—besides the subsequent editions of the *Biennale*—a profusion of events took place in Venice: Happenings, performances, and exhibitions were organized by such curators and critics as Michel Tapié; exhibitions were held in such galleries as Il Cavallino, Il Canale, Paolo Barozzi, and Il Leone; architectural conferences featured Louis Kahn, Le Corbusier, Carlo Scarpa, and Frank Lloyd Wright; fashion events were presented at Palazzo Grassi; and the city's musical life thrived with the presence of composers Bruno Maderna, Gianfrancesco Malipiero, Luigi Nono, and Goffredo Petrassi, as well as with the regular concert appearances of Leonard Bernstein, Karlheinz Stockhausen, and Igor Stravinsky. As Carrain colorfully described it, "The 1948 Biennale was like opening a bottle of Champagne. It was the explosion of modern art after the Nazis had tried to kill it."[110]

Palazzo Venier dei Leoni

In December 1948, Peggy bought the Palazzo Venier dei Leoni, an unfinished palazzo on the Grand Canal, between the Basilica of Santa Maria della Salute and the Accademia. It was designed by the Venetian architect Lorenzo Boschetti for the Veniers, an aristocratic Venetian family. Begun in 1749, only the palazzo's basement and ground floor were completed. Long and wide, it is often mistaken for a modern building and has one of the largest gardens in Venice. The word "Leoni" was added to the palazzo's name because stone lion heads were incorporated into the base of the facade, and because legend had it that in the eighteenth century a lion was kept in the garden. Interestingly, two celebrated women resided in the palazzo before Peggy: Marchesa Luisa Casati, muse of the poet Gabriele D'Annunzio, in the 1910s and 1920s, and Doris Viscountess Castlerosse in the late 1930s. The palazzo had become rather derelict by the time the Viscountess acquired it, and she installed marble bathrooms and mosaic floors. Peggy made further improvements to the house and garden, where she placed a stone "throne" on which she liked to pose for photographers. Her bedroom, painted turquoise, overlooked the Grand Canal. Over the years, she would hang exotic earrings along both sides of Alexander Calder's *Silver Bedhead* (winter 1945–46), which she had commissioned in New York. Beside Venetian mirrors, she would hang Franz von Lenbach's portraits and Francis Bacon's *Study*

for Chimpanzee (March 1957). She would display a selection of Laurence Vail's collage bottles; elsewhere in the palazzo, she kept his *Screen* (1940). The bedroom became her private retreat in the years to come when visitors strolled through the galleries in which her collection came to be installed. Or she would take refuge by sunbathing on the roof terrace during the summer months. This wing of the palazzo also contained several guest bedrooms, and the other wing had the living and dining rooms as well as the kitchen.

Peggy's collection had been brought into Italy on a temporary permit for exhibition at the *Biennale*. To avoid high import duties she would have to send the collection out of the country and then bring it back in at a lower valuation. Until such an arrangement could be made, she needed to keep the collection traveling within Italy to other exhibition venues in order to avoid being penalized by the Italian government. After she moved into the palazzo in 1949, her collection was shown in the vaulted cellar of the Palazzo Strozzi in Florence during February and March. The Palazzo Strozzi also published a catalogue.

In May 1949, Peggy decided to keep guest books. Handmade and leather bound, they are personalized with her initials, P. G., on the cover of the first book and her first name, PEGGY, on the covers of the remaining four. Leafing through them is to experience Peggy's life in Venice through the friends, art-world colleagues, and admirers who came to the palazzo—some stopped by for drinks, a meal, or a party, others as overnight guests. Her son, Sindbad, and his family inherited the guest books, among other memorabilia, after Peggy died in 1979. My mother, Peggy Angela Vail—who had married Sindbad in 1957—admired and had grown increasingly fonder of her mother-in-law over the years, even though the relationship between them had not always been easy. Peggy Angela was so intrigued by Peggy that she wished to edit and publish a selection of the best entries from the guest books. Sindbad—who had many misgivings about his family—was not overly enthusiastic about the idea but acquiesced when he better understood his wife's serious intentions. In Paris, she laboriously began to decipher signatures (many remain unidentified) and started making notes of impressions and reminiscences of Peggy and the Guggenheim-Vail family. She also discovered the previously unknown drawings sketched on pages of the guest books. Tragically, in May 1986, after many years of illness, Sindbad died of cancer. Peggy Angela had also contracted cancer, and two years later to the day, she passed away. My mother's project came to a halt, and my sister and I

Laurence Vail
Screen, 1940 (front and back)
Gouache and paper collage on canvas, mounted on wood screen, three panels, approximately 170 x 165 cm overall
Peggy Guggenheim Collection
76.2553 PG 123

inherited the guest books. I came across a pile of notes and papers relating to the books, and I decided to pursue the project in memory of my mother. When I later moved to New York, the idea of a publication and an exhibition that would encompass the many achievements of my grandmother, Peggy, sprang to mind. Within this larger project, excerpts and drawings from the guest books are published here for the first time.

Not only did Peggy acquire works of art, she also assembled guests and amassed a startling collection of their signatures, drawings, sketches, comments, reminiscences, poems, and musical bars in her guest books. Peggy took pride in these books and insisted that her guests write in them, "and if they are poets or artists they may add a poem or a drawing, which is more than welcome."[111] Although many of the artists who visited Peggy are represented in her collection, many others—who perhaps visited in the hope that she might acquire their work—are not.

The diversity of entries in the guest books makes them unique. Among others are Stella Adler, Afro, Hardy Amies, Karel Appel, Dore Ashton, Clive Bell, Isaiah Berlin, Louise Bourgeois, Marlon Brando, Art Buchwald, Bernard Buffet, Elliott Carter, Dale Chihuly, Randolph Churchill, Diana Cooper, Ian Fleming, Renato Guttuso, Patricia Highsmith, Hedda Hopper, Dominique de Menil, Eugenio Montale, Henry Moore, Gabriele Münter, Gordon Onslow-Ford, William and Babe Paley, George Plimpton, Joseph Pulitzer, Jr., Jerome Robbins, Harold Rosenberg, Anthony Armstrong-Jones (later Lord Snowdon), Karlheinz Stockhausen, Maria Talchieff, Virgil Thomson, Tennessee Williams, and Angus Wilson—all visited Peggy, leaving their names, and sometimes more, in the books. All levels of society are represented, from the builders of Peggy's *barchessa* in the garden to European aristocracy. (The Venetian aristocracy, however, did not readily accept Peggy within their community and were not intimate with her until the 1970s.) In addition to the aristocracy, Peggy enjoyed other traditional members of society, such as the officers of the United States Navy for whom she gave numerous parties over many years when they came through Venice.

The Anglo-American community in particular flocked to Peggy's, in the same way that they flocked to Harry's Bar, diagonally opposite her palazzo, on the other side of the Grand Canal. In January 1958, Al Hirschfeld would wittily depict the famous bar with Peggy in full regalia showing off her Calder earrings and heartily biting into a sandwich.

During Peggy's thirty years in the palazzo, and especially during the glamorous 1950s, one could meet all kinds of people there. The palazzo, and consequently the guest books in which so many mementos of distinguished visitors were left, symbolize Peggy's canonization as art patron and collector. She was a living legend, and her home was a cultural landmark. Visitors streamed through the palazzo mostly during the warmer months of spring and summer, and their numbers increased during the years in which a *Biennale* was held.

Some houseguests stayed for several weeks at a time, keeping Peggy and her many dogs company. The prevalence of the dog theme in the guest books might bewilder those who did not know Peggy, but her dogs were probably what she loved most. The dogs were loving and undemanding, and they truly filled an emotional gap in her life. Peggy delighted in naming her dogs, her "darling babies," as she liked to call them: Baby, Cappuccino, Emily, Foglia, Hong Kong, Madam Butterfly, Peacock, Sable, Toro, White Angel, and even Pegeen (after her daughter) and Sir Herbert (a homage to Herbert Read long before he was knighted).

The photographer Roloff Beny, who lived in Rome, was the first to write in the first guest book on May 4, 1949. Among the subsequent entries, a few weeks later, Laurence Vail wrote a few lines in verse. On the next page, Giuseppe Santomaso— a regular visitor and a neighbor who lived a few bridges away in a beautiful apartment overlooking the Grand Canal, near the Basilica of Santa Maria della Salute—was the first Venetian painter to sign the book, but he never left a sketch.

During June and July, Peggy's collection was shown in Milan's Palazzo Reale for an exhibition to benefit the Associazione Artisti d'Italia. It was so successful that the catalogue had to be reprinted. Back in Venice again, Peggy's collection was housed in the Galleria Internazionale d'Arte Moderna di Ca' Pesaro, for the Italian authorities would not allow her to take permanent possession of it. Pending the resolution of import duties, the collection remained officially in the custody of the government.

In July, Marino Marini made the first of several visits to the Palazzo Venier dei Leoni and made sketches of his trademark horses in the guest book. That month, Isamu Noguchi was among the visitors. Sindbad, referring to himself in the book as "an editor left high and dry,"[112] also visited that summer; in February, he had begun a publishing venture in Paris, a bilingual literary magazine called *Points,* dedicated to emerging

Giraffe Berto
30/6/49

YARINO

Luglio 2. 1949

Marina

Here's to you — may you give & forgive
Here's to me — may I get & forget.

Manfred Swarsenski

Peggy Guggenheim at the Palazzo
Venier dei Leoni, 1949, with sign
announcing the contemporary
sculpture exhibition held in
September and October.
© Cameraphoto–Epoche, Venice

British, American, Irish, and French writers. The collectors
Bernard and Becky Reis, Peggy's friends from New York, became
regular guests. Saul Steinberg and Hedda Sterne's first visit was
commemorated by Sterne's sketch in the guest book of Pecora,
the latest arrival among Peggy's shaggy Lhasa apsos.

With Peggy's collection still under formal control of the
Italian government, she succeeded in "borrowing" some pieces
for a sculpture exhibition held during September and October in
the palazzo's garden and terrace on the Grand Canal. Sculptures
by Pietro Consagra, Mirko (Mirko Basaldella), Salvatore
Messina, and Alberto Viani were lent directly by the artists, and
a catalogue was published for the occasion. A few plaster pieces
were displayed in the palazzo. Among the works exhibited was
Marini's *The Angel of the City* (1948, cast 1950?), which represents a man, with an erect phallus, riding a horse. Peggy had
bought the sculpture as a plaster original, and it was included in
the exhibition at the Palazzo Reale in Milan. At some point,
Peggy returned the sculpture to Marini to be cast in bronze, at
which time he made a separate phallus, "so that it could be
screwed in and out at leisure."[113] Peggy could remove it to avoid
embarrassing conservative visitors, although she would more
often than not forget to do so. After the phallus was stolen,
Marini welded a new one to the sculpture, which had been
provocatively placed on the upper terrace on the Grand Canal
across from the police headquarters of the Prefettura.

In September, such longtime friends as Nelly van Doesburg
and Mary Reynolds arrived to see Peggy. The guest book later

Pegeen
Drawing in Peggy Guggenheim's
first guest book, 1949
Ink on paper; page 22.9 x 15.6 cm
Private collection

FACING PAGE
Pavel Tchelitchew
Drawing in Peggy Guggenheim's
first guest book, 1949
Ink on paper; page 22.9 x 15.6 cm
Private collection

Miss Venice — This ancient magical object, once

Dearest Peggy — alas

Love Pauline

Venice Sept. 25. 1949.

Il n'y a aucun moyen de
mettre ce dessin en place
ce soir. Nous partons demain,
matin. Les journées sont passées
trop vite car on se sent tellement
bien. Je voudrais y revenir.
Je remercie infiniment Peggy, pour
sa gentillesse. Alberto, j'aurais

Robert Lamell

Jean Claude Winckler

that month includes entries by Leonor Fini, who drew a witty reference to her painting in Peggy's collection, *The Shepherdess of the Sphinxes* (1941), and Nancy Cunard, who merely signed. Charles Henri Ford wrote glowingly of Venice:

> Water, my element, makes a dream of air.
> Venice, gold phoenix, rises from fire,
> Her veins of sunset never know night.
> Narcissus of cities—hold tight, hold tight![114]

His companion, Pavel Tchelitchew, sketched one of his typical spiral-like heads. Pegeen also left a drawing in the guest book during this busy month.

The art historian Sam Hunter, who had met Peggy at the closing of Art of This Century in New York and was then in Venice writing for the *New York Herald Tribune*, stopped by in October. Peggy was upset that he named her "Pollock's first dealer,"[115] as she felt inadequately described; indeed, he remembers her as a prophet whose contribution to the history of American art was immense.[116]

In November, Alberto Viani signed his name in the guest book, as did Antoine Pevsner, who also wrote a grateful message. A few days later, Alberto Giacometti and his wife, Annette, spent a belated honeymoon in the palazzo. Giacometti drew a hasty pencil sketch—the only drawing of his that Peggy ever owned—and wrote in his typically modest fashion: "Il n'y a aucun moyen de mettre ce dessin en place ce soir. Nous partons demain matin. Les journées sont passées trop vite ici où je me sens tellement bien. Je voudrais y revenir, je remercie infiniment Peggy pour sa gentillesse."[117] (There is absolutely no way I can get this drawing right this evening. We are leaving tomorrow morning. The days have gone by too quickly here where I am feeling wonderful, I would like to come back, I thank Peggy so much for her kindness.)

The 1950s

The guest book entries, most limited to signatures and sometimes short comments, proliferated in the 1950s; the books that cover these years reflect the intense social life at the Palazzo Venier dei Leoni during the period. The decade began with visits from Giuseppe Santomaso and Emilio Vedova. Kenneth Macpherson, soon a regular visitor, came in May. In the guest

book, Matta drew an amusing sketch of figures kissing one another's backsides. James Lord and his companion, Bernard Minoret, visited in June, just a few days before Mark Rothko—whose sketch in Peggy's book featured a gondola—and then Barbara Hepworth and Ben Nicholson. Curator Willem Sandberg came to see Peggy to arrange an exhibition of her collection at the Stedelijk Museum in Amsterdam. A welcome visit was paid by Wyn Henderson, her assistant at Guggenheim Jeune, whose guest book entry reflects the camaraderie Peggy enjoyed with old friends: "Darling Peggy—Unlike Catullus it was to Venice and not to Sirmio I came to 'nestle in the pillow of my dreams!' The loving blessings of a renewed and regenerated Wyn Henderson."[118]

In July and August, she showed her twenty-three Jackson Pollock works, of which two were promised gifts to Amsterdam's Stedelijk Museum, in a solo exhibition—his first in Europe—at the Sala Napoleonica of the Museo Correr in Venice. The success of this exhibition—which was organized with the collaboration of Le Tre Mani (Bruno Alfieri, Oreste Ferrari, and Giuseppe Marchiori) and Vittorio Carrain—delighted Peggy, who wrote,

Eugene Berman
Drawing in Peggy Guggenheim's
first guest book, 1950
Ink and pencil on paper; page 22.9 x
15.6 cm
Private collection

FACING PAGE

Peggy Guggenheim on the roof terrace
of the Palazzo Venier dei Leoni,
photographed in 1950 by David Seymour
for Magnum Photos.
Collection of Kathy McCarver and
Steven Mnuchin

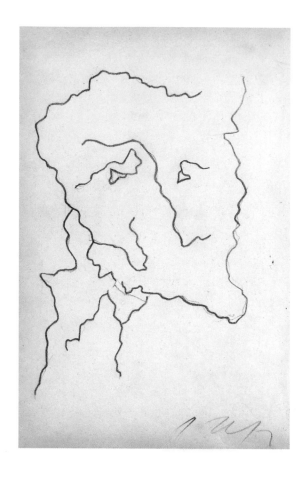

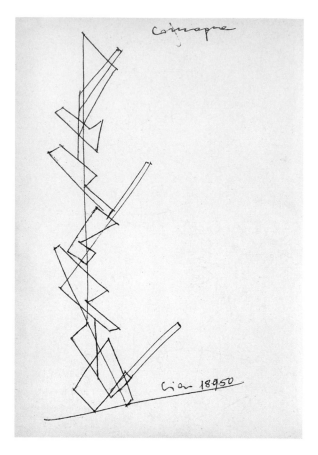

"It seemed to place Pollock historically where he belonged as one of the greatest painters of our time."[119] She also organized Jean Hélion's solo exhibition, held during August and September, at the Sala degli Specchi in the Palazzo Giustinian.

In August, on facing pages of the guest book, Jean Arp left an organic sketch, and Graham Sutherland, visiting Peggy for the first time, drew a praying mantis. When Sutherland visited Peggy in the 1960s, he insisted that she return a painting of his that she had recently bought but which he considered inferior; he subsequently replaced it with *Organic Form* (1962–68). In September, Alfred Frankfurter, who had organized an exhibition in the *Biennale*'s American pavilion, which included three paintings by Pollock, was a guest as was Truman Capote, on the first of several visits. During this period, artist and stage designer Eugene Berman drew the first of his witty sketches of Peggy's dogs in the guest books; it shows a winged Lhasa apso perched on top of a tall Greek column, an allusion to the statue of a winged lion, symbol of Venice, that towers over the square between the Palazzo Ducale and piazza San Marco. On the same day in September, Gino Severini and Pietro

Souvenir d'une
bella journée à Venise
chez Madame Guggenheim
G. Severini
18 Sept. 1950.

Peggy Guggenheim in her bedroom at the
Palazzo Venier dei Leoni, early 1950s.
Private collection.
© Cameraphoto–Epoche, Venice

FACING PAGE

Marc Chagall
Drawing in Peggy Guggenheim's
first guest book, 1950
Ink on paper; page 22.9 x 15.6 cm
Private collection

Consagra left ink drawings in the book. At the end of the month,
John Rothenstein, director of the Tate Gallery, visited.

Peggy lent Carlo Cardazzo several of her Pollock paintings
for a solo exhibition at his Milan gallery, Il Naviglio, during
October and November. October brought Bruno Cagli and Marc
Chagall, who drew an emblematic face in Peggy's guest book, to
the palazzo. That month, Sandberg again visited Peggy in antici-
pation of showing her collection in Amsterdam; the exhibition
opened at the Stedelijk Museum in January 1951 and traveled
to the Palais des Beaux-Arts in Brussels and then to the
Kunsthaus Zürich. From Zurich, the collection was sent back to
Italy. Peggy wrote, "It was all very easy. . . . they [the artworks]
were brought in at four o'clock in the morning—an Alpine pass.
These very stupid, sleepy *douaniers*, who didn't know what
it was all about, let them come in for I think $1000."[120] In this
manner, Peggy was finally able to permanently move her
collection into the palazzo.

In 1951, Peggy's collection was installed throughout the
palazzo; the courtyard became a sculpture garden. From the
spring into the fall, the collection could be seen, free of charge,
by the public on three afternoons a week. The architectural
firm BBPR (Lodovico Barbiano di Belgiojoso, Enrico Peressutti,
and Ernesto Nathan Rogers) presented a plan for the restoration
of her palazzo and additional exhibition space, conceiving,
according to Peggy, "a two-story gallery elevated from my roof
on pillars twenty feet high. The front was to resemble the Doge's
Palace, and in their minds they [BBPR] conceived something that
they thought would be a link between the past and the
present."[121] Peggy disliked the design and decided against it. In
the early 1950s, with the help of Matta, Peggy turned the basement rooms into galleries.

Ken Scott, who had exhibited as a painter (Kenneth Scott) at
Art of This Century and was now a fashion designer, visited
in early spring, as did W. Somerset Maugham, who wrote in
the guest book to acknowledge a "perfect dry Martini."[122] Saul
Steinberg and Hedda Sterne were back in May. In June,
Philip Johnson wrote that Peggy's palazzo was "the only place
I would trade for the Glass House,"[123] his New Canaan,
Connecticut, home. The English aesthete and writer Harold
Acton—whose own home, Villa La Pietra, in Florence was anoth-
er famous Anglo-American gathering place—was "intoxicated
by the achievements of mine hostess,"[124] alluding not only to her
artistic accomplishments but also to her sexual ones, perhaps

A
Peggy

Marc

Chagall

1950

envying her for her many male conquests. In September, Stephen Spender, who would visit regularly, was one of many guests. Wifredo Lam drew a small dragon in the guest book in December, and an appreciative Nelly van Doesburg filled a whole page, dated November–December, effusively thanking Peggy for her loving care while van Doesburg was sick. In August, Peggy had met Raoul Gregorich, twenty-three years her junior. A good companion, uncomplicated, and quite uninterested in and ignorant about art, he became a frequent guest and was Peggy's last great love.

Peggy's second guest book begins in late December 1951 with a colorful watercolor by Roloff Beny. In early 1952, on the recommendation of William Congdon, Peggy became the patron of Tancredi (Parmeggiani Tancredi), a young artist living in Venice. Tancredi soon began an affair with Peggy's daughter, Pegeen, who would remain married to Jean Hélion until 1958. Peggy gave Tancredi—an adherent of the artists' group Movimento Spaziale, which had been founded by Lucio Fontana—use of a basement studio in the palazzo as well as a stipend until 1955. Eleven Tancredi works acquired by Peggy remain in the collection. Over the years, her support of Italian artists included the purchase of works by Edmondo Bacci, Consagra, Piero Dorazio, Mirko, Santomaso, and Vedova, among many others. Although she focused on buying Italian art, she also bought works by artists as diverse as Pierre Alechinsky, Francis Bacon, Congdon, Alan Davie, Willem de Kooning, Jean Dubuffet, and Mark Tobey.

June 1952 brought the *Biennale*, and with it many friends, such as Elsa Schiaparelli and Herbert Read, who wrote in the guest book, quoting T. S. Eliot's *The Family Reunion*, "You and I / My dear, may very likely meet again / In our wanderings in the neutral territory / Between two worlds."[125] Read would visit regularly through the years during the *Biennale* season. At this time, he and Alfred H. Barr, Jr., stayed at the palazzo for a few weeks. A drawing by Friedensreich Hundertwasser is followed by one by Afro (Afro Basaldella), which is signed "Afro . . . il cow-boy."[126]

In August, Paul Bowles stayed for a few weeks in the palazzo. His entry in the guest book begins "for Mrs. Bowles," includes a musical bar, and then closes with "New York, the non-Jewish lake, Easthampton, Venice."[127] His words recall the time in the 1940s when Bowles had helped Peggy obtain a lease on a country house under the names "Mr. and Mrs. Bowles"; as

To Peggy, STEINBERG
May, 1951

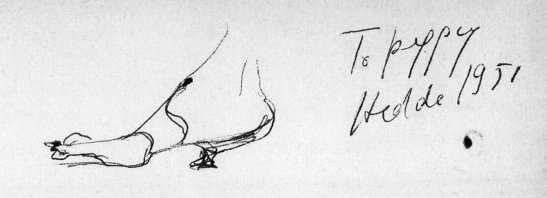

To pppy 1951
Hellde 1951

27 - maggio 951   San Romano

There was a young girl of Madras
Who walked into the water up to her ankles.
That doesn't rhyme now, but wait till the tide comes in.
                    Richard McComb Martin
                         27/v/51.

Reusto CAREZZO
—
With many thanks for a delightful
introduction to Venice & the Grand Canal —
                    Barney Blair

Very sorry but I'm just not very clever,
but it's much fun.
                    Ginny Blair

a Jew, she would have been denied the rental. Perhaps such
memories played some part in her generous donation, through
the American Fund for Israel Institutions, of thirty-four
paintings—including works by William Baziotes, Max Ernst,
Hélion, André Masson, Man Ray, and Pollock—to the Tel-Aviv
Museum in 1952; indeed, of the many gifts she gave to museums
around the world, this was to be her second-largest donation to a
single institution. Eugene Kolb, chief curator of the museum,
wrote, "It has been the purpose of this gift—for which we cannot
be grateful enough—to encourage the creation of a special collection of abstract and surrealist art in our Museum."[128]

In September, Joan Miró sketched a delightful constellation-
like form in the guest book. At the end of the month, Hans
Hartung drew sketches on two pages and Capote as well as
Read, again quoting from Eliot's *The Family Reunion*,
reappeared. As would be the general rule, the autumn and
winter months were quiet; Peggy's collection was closed to
the public, and there were fewer foreigners in Venice during
these seasons.

Peggy Guggenheim and Caresse
Crosby, photographed in Venice
by Roloff Beny.
Roloff Beny Collection, Documentary
Art and Photography Division,
National Archives of Canada, Ottawa

FACING PAGE

Victor Brauner
Drawing in Peggy Guggenheim's
second guest book, 1954
Watercolor on paper; page 22.9 x
15.9 cm
Private collection

In March 1953, Laurence Vail and his companion, Yvonne
Hagen, the art columnist for the *International Herald Tribune*,
were among Peggy's visitors; Laurence's wife, Jean Connolly, had
died in 1952. A friend from the Paris and New York days,
Caresse Crosby—who had fostered many writers through the
Black Sun Press in 1920s–30s Paris—became a frequent guest
and often accompanied Peggy in her gondola. Some guest book
entries are all the more extraordinary in that several notable
personalities visited at the same time; for example, Cecil Beaton,
Capote, and Matta, who wrote, "beware of the 'never man'
sometimes it 'appears' as a tru man,"[129] all appear on one page
from this summer. During his visit in September, Sam Francis
wrote the exquisite line: "White is the space between."[130] The
next day—nearly three years later to the day since his previous
visit—Frankfurter was at the palazzo. In the autumn, John
Richardson and the actor Farley Granger also returned.

In April 1954, Tancredi and Pegeen were guests.
Subsequently, Max Ernst—who was being awarded the painting
prize at the *Biennale*—and his wife, Dorothea Tanning, visited.
Tanning sketched Peggy's dogs in the book, and Max wrote,

A PEGGY EN SOUVENIR,
D'UN RÊVE DEVENU RÉEL,
D'UNE SOMPTUEUSE
HOSPITALITÉE
          GRANDE,
D'UNE HAUTEUR D'ESPRIT
ET D'ART INEPUISABLE,
MES REMERCIEMENTS,
VICTOR BRAUNER
2.6. JUIN 1954,—

"peace for ever un vrai ami est revenu for ever Contre signé darling Peggy"[131] (peace for ever a real friend has come back for ever counter signed darling Peggy). Max was now a welcome visitor at the palazzo, and he and Victor Brauner spent much time in Peggy's garden playing with her dogs. As always, summer during a *Biennale* was the busiest time, with visits from curators and collectors, as well as such artists as Karel Appel, Arp, Robert Brady, Matta, Marino Marini, and David Smith. Clare Booth Luce, the United States ambassador to Italy from 1953 to 1956, whom Peggy described "as usual, was very polite and charming, and of course marvelously dressed, looking younger and more glamorous than ever,"[132] visited one evening. Luce appeared to like Pegeen's paintings best because of or despite the fact that she thought the people in them appeared to have "nothing to say."[133] Arp and his wife, Marguerite, stayed with Peggy for a few days and were delighted to ride in her gondola. In the guest book, Brauner left a beautiful watercolor reference to his painting *The Surrealist* (January 1947) in Peggy's collection. In July, on "the day after Independence Day,"[134] Richardson and his companion, collector Douglas Cooper, visited; Cooper lamented a "very very bad Biennale" but was comforted by "pictures in your palazzo which are real works of art."[135]

Composers Ned Rorem and Goffredo Petrassi each left a musical bar on a page together. Many years later, Rorem described Peggy as having been "rather grand, aware of herself,

stunning without beauty . . . a force in the world of art."[136]
Helen Frankenthaler and Clement Greenberg were guests in
September 1954. Peggy would travel with them to Milan.
Frankenthaler has fondly recalled Peggy's "somewhat camou-
flaged diction" and that she was a "queen who ran a rather formal palazzo and entertained in Guggenheim style on the Grand
Canal."[137] Greenberg sketched a gondola in the guest book and
wrote, "To Peggy, who's transferred her light from N.Y. to Venice,
to the former's infinite loss and the latter's infinite gain."[138]

After Gregorich died in a car accident in September, Peggy
felt devastated.[139] Sometime in late fall or in early winter
1954–55, having decided to get away, she went first to Ceylon to
visit Paul and Jane Bowles. She then set off alone for India,
where she "visited over twenty cities in forty-eight days,"[140]
including trips to museums and artists' studios. She was disap-
pointed with the contemporary art in Ceylon and India but was
impressed by Chandigarh, the new capital of the Punjab, which
included designs by Le Corbusier. During her travels, she bought
many fanciful earrings, and in Darjeeling visited Tenzing
Norkay, not so much because he had climbed Mount Everest
with Edmund Hillary, but rather because of her interest in his
long-haired Lhasa apsos.

With Peggy back in Venice in early 1955, guests again came
to the palazzo. Giulio Turcato and Edmondo Bacci were among
the artists who visited. Peggy would help sell Bacci's works to

Tancredi
Drawing in Peggy Guggenheim's
third guest book, 1955
Ink, watercolor, and gouache on paper;
page 22.9 x 15.6 cm
Private collection

FOLLOWING TWO PAGES

Matta
Drawing in Peggy Guggenheim's
second guest book, 1954
Pencil and crayon on paper; page 22.9 x
15.9 cm
Private collection

lay etc-etros and the myth fit —
diffucis per colla Jubis

Paquita : your nanny

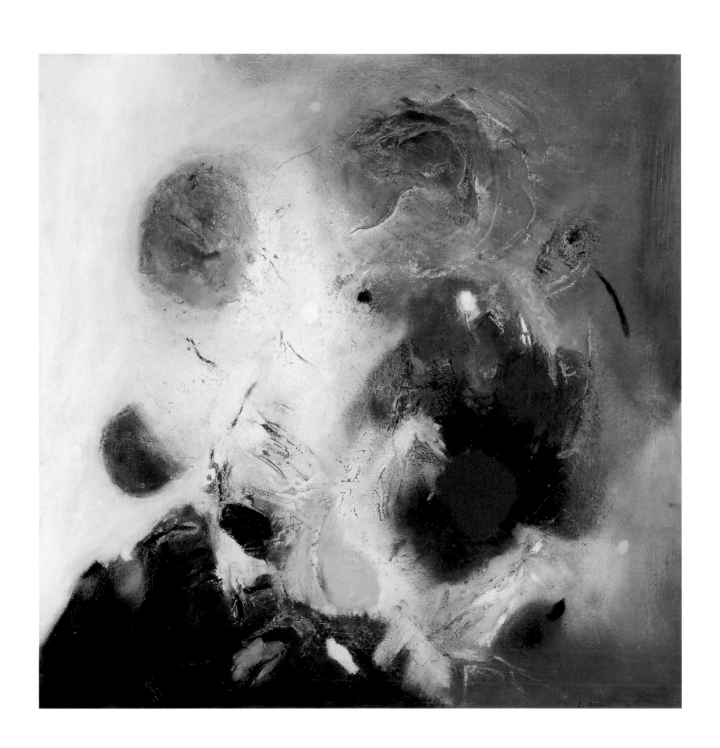

other collectors and keep two of his paintings, including *Event #247* (1956), for her collection. In the catalogue of Bacci's solo exhibition at Carlo Cardazzo's gallery Il Cavallino in 1957, she wrote, "Each new work is more vital than the previous one. I feel they are so explosive that they put in danger the security of my palazzo. Each time that an American enthusiast takes one away, I feel that my house is in a less dangerous predicament. But then, Bacci brings me a new one. Each one is more marvellous, more exciting and more dangerous."[141]

Peggy could be generous and gracious spontaneously and often unexpectedly, but she could also be selfish, cold, and manipulative. In the third guest book, which begins in May 1955, Sindbad, as he often did, wrote a poem:

Indeed it is hard
to be an eternal bard
To tax one's imagination
is a perpetual frustration
It is also banal
To talk of a canal
or love and sex
as an eternal hex
What a pity
to be witty
without the ability.
Je ne puis écrire plus
Car je dois garder un surplus
pour mon proche retour
A cette ville où on ne trouve pas toujours L'AMOUR.[142]

The last four lines—I cannot write anymore / because I must keep a surplus / for my next visit / to this town where one does not always find love—in particular suggest Sindbad's both tender and caustic feelings for his mother.

Hans Richter was a frequent guest; in recent years, he had been working on the Venetian episode of his film *8 x 8* (1957). Buffie Johnson, who had participated in *31 Women* at Art of This Century, was living at the time in Venice and was a regular at Peggy's memorable parties. Johnson, who first met Peggy in Paris before World War II, has remembered her behaving like a queen and rather impatient in manner.[143] Visitors in the fall included Consagra, Mary McCarthy, and Jack Youngerman.

In spring 1956, poet Alan Ansen made his first visit; in 1959, he would put on the first of three masques in Peggy's garden. Spender, visiting in March, hoped to be mentioned in the second volume of her autobiography should one appear, and novelist Alberto Moravia paid a visit together with art historian Giovanni Carandente. A "reciprocal intellectual fire"[144] ensued, and she talked with Moravia about literature, perhaps her true passion, for hours. For his Cavallino editions, Carlo Cardazzo asked Peggy to write a book of anecdotes, which Laurence Vail entitled *Una collezionista ricorda* (1956); the dust jacket shows Peggy with Alexander Calder's *Silver Bedhead* and surrounded by eight Lhasa apsos. Capote arrived in May and stayed for six weeks while he wrote *The Muses Are Heard* (1956), his nonfiction account of the American touring company of George Gershwin's *Porgy and Bess* (1935), whose itinerary had included the opera's Italian premiere in Venice in September 1955. In 1961, on the same page as his 1956 guest book entry, Capote would return "to sign this memory of 5 years ago."[145]

That year's *Biennale* visitors started to come to Peggy's palazzo, and one of the first was Katharine Kuh; now a curator at the Art Institute of Chicago, she had organized *The American Painters and the City* for the American pavilion. Lynn Chadwick, recipient of the sculpture prize, visited Peggy as did Alberto Giacometti for the first time since 1949. Other guests included Jean Cocteau, a friend since Guggenheim Jeune days. The signatures of George Balanchine, whose calligraphy sprawls, nearly dancing, across the page, and Anthony Caro, whose handwriting is tidy and cramped, appear on one page of the guest book in September. In October, Thomas Messer, not yet the third director of the Solomon R. Guggenheim Museum, paid the first of many visits.

The first few months of 1957 were relatively quiet until the arrival of Claire Falkenstein, who a few years later designed the beautiful *Entrance Gates to the Palazzo* (1961) for the palazzo's *calle* (alleyway) entrance. Art historian Leo Steinberg wrote in the guest book that Peggy's palazzo was "the only house in Venice that does not make one feel ashamed to be of this century."[146] Margaret Scolari Barr had instructed Steinberg on how to handle Peggy when he visited her: "She will certainly take you for a ride in her gondola, and then, if she takes your hand, I suggest you let her, on the principle of ça coûte si peu et ça donne tellement de plaisir! [it costs so little and it gives so much pleasure!]"[147] There was no need to accommodate Peggy in

Truman Capote on the roof terrace of the Palazzo Venier dei Leoni, 1950s. Private collection

FACING PAGE

Jean Cocteau
Drawing in Peggy Guggenheim's third guest book, 1956
Ink on paper; page 22.9 x 15.6 cm
Private collection

Jean Cocteau
× 1956
vers

this respect, however, because she began to complain about an art museum to which she had given a Pollock painting. Now that the Pollock had become so valuable, she wished to retrieve it. Steinberg, who advised her to take pride in what she had done to promote Pollock's work, was pleasantly surprised by her enthusiasm for and knowledge of Venetian art and culture. He was delighted that a collector of Modern and contemporary art should be so taken with classical Italian art.[148]

Igor Stravinsky signed the guest book with musical bars at the end of September, but composer Luigi Nono only left his signature. In July, Allen Ginsberg wrote to Peggy in a letter:

> Thank you for saying OK on my coming to your house tomorrow night. I've never been in a great formal historic salon before & naturally have been eager to go there, be accepted, see pictures at leisure, sip big cocktails, gaze over grand canal, be a poet in Venice surrounded by famous ladies, echoes of Partisan Review & the 20's & surrealists, butlers & gondolas, enjoy a little fame and escape the illusion of poverty—all tempting, especially the sense of acceptance.[149]

He paid at least one visit that summer, but neither a signature nor poem has been found in the guest book. At the end of the year, Alec Guinness visited Peggy as did the art historians John Fleming and Hugh Honour.

The poet Gregory Corso, one of the few visitors in January 1958, left a drawing and a poem in the guest book:

> And she, her ruminating deer,
> 2 thousand years old,
> hath hired sight not for sordid cameo—
> but a quiet room of earrings.
> But Bacon screams a melting Baboon
>   across the bed!
> The butterfly spectacles tremble!
> O but does not the frenzy of Pollock
>   downstairs add to the dumb of earrings?
> Picasso and Arp seem angry at each other—
>   Arp in the yard bends tonight—
>   Picasso laughs in the too-much light.
> And poor Ernst—his birdy girls are taloned old.
> And all the canvasses grow sea lonely sure.
> And with deep metamorphical gondola eyes

I see Venice as Death and would embrace it
were't [sic] it not for an ever constant cry
of gold in the peace of Parisian noon.[150]

The winter months were quiet in Venice and work was under way to build a *barchessa*—the Venetian word for a place in which to store grain and hay—in the garden to provide additional galleries for Peggy's collection. The *barchessa* was built— along the depth of the garden—at a ninety-degree angle to the end of the palazzo's bedroom wing. Venetian authorities consented to the new structure with the provision that a substantial portion of the garden should separate the new structure from the main house. However, only a small area of the garden was kept between the two structures, and today the *barchessa* is linked to the palazzo by a passageway. The architect Vincenzo Passero was urged to have the *barchessa* ready in time for the *Biennale*. Peggy gave the workmen a dinner party in her favorite restaurant, and she asked them all to write in the guest book. Passero made a drawing of the *barchessa*, and one workman wrote a poem in Venetian dialect, in which he called Peggy "Leonessa" in honor of the name of her palazzo. Peggy herself wrote in the book that this evening had been "the nicest night of my life in Venice 1946–1958."[151]

In the spring, James Lord and Bernard Minoret brought Dora Maar with them to visit Peggy. As Lord wrote:

It seemed fitting that two ladies who had in one way or another made themselves important to the art of their era should come face to face. Peggy was always content to parade her pictures and I thought she'd be flattered to have under her roof a woman who had so often inspired Picasso. The meeting was not a success, because both ladies liked being catered to, though not at all in the same manner. When we left the Palazzo Venier dei Leoni, Dora said: "Madame Guggenheim merits our compassion, but she wouldn't know how to go about being worthy of it." Bernard asked what that meant, and Dora replied, "That's the mystery."[152]

The 1958 *Biennale* brought such visitors to the palazzo as Cocteau, the curator William Lieberman, gallery owner André Emmerich, Antoine Pevsner, and Sutherland. In early 1959, Peggy went to Mexico and from there to New York for the first time since 1948. She was in New York when Frank Lloyd Wright died in April. She visited with friends and family, including Harry Guggenheim, who gave her a tour of Wright's nearly completed building for the Solomon R. Guggenheim Museum. Peggy described Wright's building as "a huge garage . . . It is built on a site that is inadequate for its size and looks very cramped, suffering from its nearness to adjacent buildings. . . . Around an enormous space intended for sculpture displays, the rising ramp, Wright's famous invention, coils like an evil serpent."[153] Her old friend James Johnson Sweeney was now the museum's director.

One of Peggy's favorite excursions in America was visiting the Philadelphia Museum of Art, where she could once again see Walter and Louise Arensberg's collection, and the Barnes Foundation, just outside Philadelphia. Peggy found the New York art world very changed and could not afford to buy contemporary art, so she began to buy pre-Columbian, African, and Oceanic art. She would write, "In fact, I do not like art today. I think it has gone to hell, as a result of the financial attitude."[154] She went on to say:

> One cannot expect every decade to produce genius. The twentieth century has already produced enough. We should not expect anymore. A field must lie fallow every now and then. Artists try too hard to be original. That is why we have all this painting that isn't painting any more. For the moment we should content ourselves with what the twentieth century has produced. . . . Today is the age of collecting, not of creation. Let us at least preserve and present to the masses all the great treasures we have.[155]

Peggy was back in Venice by May. During the spring and summer, such personalities as the poet James Merrill and art historian Robert Rosenblum visited her. She also had a fond reunion with Frederick Kiesler. When Georges Mathieu exhibited at Il Cavallino, he visited Peggy in September and sketched an energetic drawing, in his typical gestural fashion, in the guest book.

The 1960s

Spring 1960 brought a visit from Justin K. Thannhauser and his wife, Hilde, generous donors to the Solomon R. Guggenheim

Museum. Friends came to the Palazzo Venier dei Leoni during the summer, but the guest books contain surprisingly few entries during those months. In a letter to Robert Brady, Peggy described the *Biennale* as "worse than ever and Fautrier got the biggest prize. He is undoubtedly the worst painter in the Biennale. . . . I have never seen such a horrible Biennale. Also it is more and more like a big money art market and absolutely everyone was here."[156] In September, Marcel Duchamp was welcomed to the palazzo, as were composer John Cage, choreographer Merce Cunningham, dancer Carolyn Brown, and composer David Tudor. Cage was a celebrity in Italy, and Cunningham wrote in the guest book about the wonderful parties Peggy gave for him and his entourage: "party!! party!! all marvelous!!"[157] In the book, Cage filled two pages with musical bars and his recollections of his arrival in New York in 1942:

> When Xenia [then his wife] and I came to New York from Chicago, we arrived in the Bus Station with about 25 cents. We were invited to stay for a while with you and Max Ernst. Max Ernst had met us in Chicago and had said: "Whenever you come to New York, come and stay with us. We have a big house on the East River." I went to the phone booth in the Bus Station, put in a nickel, and dialed. Max Ernst answered. He didn't recognize my voice. Finally he said, "Are you thirsty?" I said, "Yes." He said: "Well, come over tomorrow for cocktails." I went back to Xenia and told her what had happened. She said: "Call him back. We have everything to gain and nothing to lose." I did. He said, "Oh! It's you. We've been waiting for you for weeks. Your room's ready. Come right over." East River 1942, Grand Canal September 1960 (con La Fenice!)."[158]

In spring 1961, Truman Capote was delighted to be at Peggy's again. In May, Man Ray, whom Peggy had not seen for many years, came to visit, and his friend and fellow Dadaist, Tristan Tzara, whom Peggy had known in Paris in the 1920s, arrived a few days later. In the summer, many regular guests came, as well as a newcomer, the curator Sam Wagstaff (later famous for his photography collection).

In October, Giacometti came to visit Peggy and wrote in her guest book. The director Joseph Losey was in Venice in December working on his film *Eve* (1962), which starred Jeanne Moreau. He asked Peggy to play an extra. All she had to do was sit at a gambling table, for which she was paid a fee of 80,000 lire, or $125 at the time. That same month, Giorgio Albertazzi, who had just starred in Alain Resnais's *Last Year at Marienbad* (1961) visited. During 1961, Claire Falkenstein's *Entrance Gates to the Palazzo*, "wrought-iron gates with brilliant lumps of colored glass trapped in the mesh,"[159] were installed at the palazzo.

In early January 1962, Peggy participated in a RAI television series about the joys of Venice in winter. Ugo Mulas took photographs for Michelangelo Muraro's book *Invito a Venezia* (1962; published in English as *Invitation to Venice* in 1963), and Peggy wrote the introduction, in which she conveyed her love for the city. She wrote that "to live in Venice or even to visit it means that you fall in love with the city itself. There is nothing left over in your heart for anyone else."[160]

Albertazzi returned in early February and inaugurated the fourth guest book. It was during this month that Peggy was made an honorary citizen of Venice. She wore an extravagant black-plumed hat for the occasion and was presented with a certificate and magnificent roses at the town hall. Giuseppe Santomaso and Emilio Vedova were the only artists to attend the ceremony. It was not until the summer that the *Biennale* attracted such old friends as Nelly van Doesburg and E. L. T.

Peggy Guggenheim and Nelly van Doesburg in the living room of the Palazzo Venier dei Leoni, photographed by Roloff Beny. Roloff Beny Collection, Documentary Art and Photography Division, National Archives of Canada, Ottawa

FACING PAGE

Man Ray
Drawing in Peggy Guggenheim's third guest book, 1961
Ink and postage stamp on paper; page 22.9 x 15.6 cm
Private collection

Man

Ray

avec les arrières pensées de
may 10 1961   man Ray

Mesens. In the fall, she went to Japan, where she traveled with Cage, Tudor, and Yoko Ono, who accompanied them as a translator. (In later years, Ono and John Lennon would visit Peggy several times, but they did not sign the guest book or leave any sketches.)

In February 1963, Irene Rice Pereira and Peggy Waldman, a friend since childhood, came to see Peggy. In October, Claire Falkenstein was back to repair the gates. That same month, and just a few days after the opening of her exhibition at Galerie Laurence in Paris, Helen Frankenthaler came to the palazzo, "nine years later,"[161] as she noted in the guest book. She was

Cecil Beaton
Drawing in Peggy Guggenheim's
fourth guest book, 1965
Ink on paper; page 22.9 x 15.6 cm
Private collection

116

accompanied by Robert Motherwell, then her husband, who acknowledged Peggy as his "first patron"[162] and made a small sketch in the style of his series *Elegies to the Spanish Republic*.

In January 1964, Peggy went to London to celebrate Herbert Read's seventieth birthday. Beginning that April, few drawings appear in the guest books. Peggy described the year's *Biennale* as dull, but not quite as dull as the one in 1962; she felt, however, that Robert Rauschenberg deserved to win the painting prize. Jean Dubuffet was a visitor as were Lee Miller and her husband, Roland Penrose. The Venetian glass artist Egidio Costantini also visited, and twenty-three of his glass sculptures after sketches by Picasso (1964) as well as *Clementine* (1966), a collaboration with Pegeen, would enter Peggy's collection.

Amid yet another slow winter, Peggy lent her entire collection to the Tate Gallery at the invitation of its director, Norman Reid. She traveled to London for the exhibition, which opened at the very end of December and was shown until March 1965. It was a special triumph for Peggy because in 1938 the Tate's then director, James B. Manson, had refused to certify that sculptures destined for a Guggenheim Jeune exhibition were art. Now, she was being courted by the Tate, which published a catalogue for the occasion. By the spring, the collection was back at the palazzo, and spring and summer saw the return of faithful guests as well as Rex Harrison and a German television crew, which made a documentary on Peggy.

In March 1966, Charmion von Wiegand was delighted "to see the richly textured and complex collection again and to remember the old days in New York."[163] In June, Marcel Duchamp, visiting with his wife, Teeny, found it "délicieux de voir Peggy sans préméditation"[164] (delicious to see Peggy without premeditation). Françoise Gilot and Max Ernst were also among the visitors that month. A dinner party was held at the restaurant La Fenice in honor of Peggy and Max. Dinner guests included Norman Reid and Wilhelm Sandberg, two museum directors vying for Peggy's collection. Peggy and Max sat next to each other, both older, white-haired, and distinguished. Pegeen sketched her last drawing in a guest book. Curator Pontus Hulten visited in September to make arrangements for Peggy's collection to travel to the Moderna Museet in Stockholm.

November was a particularly tragic month in Venice in the aftermath of the disastrous floods that devastated Venice and Florence. Peggy would remember this Christmas as very

TOP

Peggy Guggenheim and John Cage in Japan, 1962.
Private collection

BOTTOM

Alberto Giacometti and Peggy Guggenheim at the Venice *Biennale*, 1962.
La Biennale di Venezia, Archivio Storico delle Arti Contemporanee

quiet, without even a tree in piazza San Marco. In December,
Peggy was made a *commendatore* of the Italian republic.
That month, Peggy went to Stockholm for the exhibition of her
collection, which would be held from November 1966 to January
1967; she was King Gustav Adolf's guide at the opening. The
exhibition, which had an accompanying catalogue, traveled to
the Louisiana Museum of Modern Art in Humlebaek, Denmark.
After spending a few days in Denmark, Peggy went to visit
Robert Brady in Mexico at the end of February; it was there that
she got the tragic news of Pegeen's death from an overdose
of barbiturates in Paris. Upon her return to Venice, Peggy made
alterations to the palazzo's galleries and dedicated a memorial
room solely to Pegeen and her paintings.

April, as usual, saw the return of longtime friends, as well as
the visit of the poet Seamus Heaney and his family. Heaney,
"overawed by the whole evening," has remembered "Peggy showing us the little rhyme which James Joyce had written in the
flyleaf of a book: a cunning bit of doggerel, punning bilingually
on Joyce's chronic inability to be going home early and the word
Guggenheim."[165] It was a relatively quiet summer, and Peggy
was still in shock over Pegeen's death.

Roloff Beny persuaded Peggy to accompany him to India
in early 1968. She and Beny, whose relationship was as special
as it was durable, traveled extensively in India. Peggy was
unspoiled in terms of creature comforts, and they stayed in
places ranging from small canvas tents to huts in villages to

Maharajahs' palaces. She adored Indian food and was particularly fond of popadum, a light waferlike bread. Because of its cheap price and light weight, she ordered a huge quantity to be shipped to her palazzo. A gondola load duly arrived, and over two years later Peggy was still diligently eating her way through the popadum, which should have been crisp but had become damp and stale.

In April, Laurence Vail died in the south of France. That spring Bernard Malamud was among the visitors to the palazzo. Fewer artists and more European socialites came to visit during this particular *Biennale*; indeed, the student protests of 1968 had led to many artists refusing to take part in the *Biennale*. Peggy went only once to this *Biennale* and saw little that interested her besides works by Marisol (Marisol Escobar) and Rufino Tamayo. She cared less and less for contemporary art although she claimed to like Jasper Johns and Robert Rauschenberg; she said, "I wanted to buy Rauschenberg's goat with a tire around it [*Monogram*, 1955–59, now in the collection of the Moderna Museet, Stockholm] for my grandchildren,"[166] but she did not buy any of his works. In October, Norton Simon visited Peggy and asked her whether she would leave her collection to the University of California, Berkeley. She retorted that she would if he saved Venice; she never heard from him again.

In January 1969, Peggy arrived in New York, where a selection of works from her collection was exhibited at the Solomon R. Guggenheim Museum from January to March. A catalogue was published for the exhibition. Thomas Messer, director of the museum since 1961, was in the midst of a long term courtship of Peggy for the disposition of her collection. Thanks to the patient efforts of Messer, Peggy came to make peace with her father's family. When Peggy was back in Venice that spring Gore Vidal, an old friend, and S. I. Newhouse, a first-time guest were among her visitors.

The 1970s

Fewer guests came to see Peggy in the 1970s, and of those most were familiar faces. Robert Graves was among the few new visitors. Spring and summer brought Farley Granger and Isamu Noguchi, who inscribed his sketch in the guest book as "Merlin's circle into which we will disappear."[167] In February 1972, the British consul Ashley Clarke and his wife made the first of many visits. Giuseppe Santomaso was one of the few artists who came to see Peggy during this period. John Hohnsbeen, Peggy's new assistant, provided her with much-needed companionship. In May, Peggy traveled to Florence with Roloff Beny to see the Henry Moore retrospective at Forte Belvedere. The fourth guest book concludes in June 1972 with signatures of faithful friends. By this time, Peggy was disillusioned with the art world, and younger artists either snubbed her or felt snubbed by her.

The fifth and final guest book consists almost entirely of signatures. The book covers the period from mid-June 1972 until October 1979, a few months before Peggy's death. Time passed by quickly in the books, even if it did not do so for an older and sadder Peggy. Many of the old guard, as well as a few newcomers, continued to visit Peggy. Sindbad continued to make regular trips to Venice to see her, and she occasionally came to Paris to see him and her grandchildren. Spring and summer 1973 brought visits from Beny, now celebrating twenty-five years of friendship with Peggy, and Cecil Beaton, who returned for the last time and sketched a figure in the guest book. In April 1974, Brassaï (Gyula Halász) came to see her. Among Peggy's visitors in June were European aristocracy and royalty; Françoise Gilot and her husband, Jonas Salk; collector Eugene V. Thaw, coauthor of Jackson Pollock's catalogue raisonné; and Thomas Messer. Messer, having at last secured the disposition of Peggy's collection for the Solomon R. Guggenheim Foundation, expressed his "gratitude for my longest, best and most fruitful stay to date!"[168] By 1976, the Palazzo Venier dei Leoni and her collection were transferred to the control of the foundation, which agreed that she would continue to live there, and that upon her death the collection would remain in place.

From December 1974 to March 1975, Peggy's collection was exhibited in Paris at the Orangerie des Tuileries. A catalogue was published, and the exhibition was very successful, but Peggy writes in her memoirs that she was treated with little courtesy and that everyone was "terribly disagreeable."[169] From December 1975 to February 1976, Peggy's collection was shown at the Galleria Civica d'Arte Moderna di Torino, which published an exhibition catalogue. Peggy disliked the installation but was delighted with the reception from the Communist mayor, who offered her "caviar and smoked salmon sandwiches."[170]

Peggy's eightieth birthday party, on August 26, 1978, was organized by Jane Rylands—whose husband, Philip, would later become deputy director of the Peggy Guggenheim

Collection—and hosted by Nico Passante, the hotel's director, at the Gritti Hotel, just across the canal from the palazzo. The guests included Sindbad and Peggy Angela, Ashley Clarke, Joseph Losey, and a few close friends. The "ultima Dogaressa," as she had come to be called, was celebrated with a beautiful white cake in the shape of her palazzo. At the end of December, Emilio Vedova paid an unexpected visit to wish Peggy a happy new year.

In May 1979, Peggy was delighted to see Vidal again, who had come with Paul Newman and Joanne Woodward. Peggy was especially thrilled when Newman agreed to kiss one of her maids, believing that as a consequence the maid would stay in her employment for at least another year.[171] The Australian prime minister, Gough Whitlam also visited at this time. Fond comments characterize the final pages of the last guest book. Peggy's cousin, the archaeologist Iris Love called her "the one member of the family I most admire, and one of the people I most respect in the world."[172]

In October, Jimmy Ernst and his wife, Dallas, were the last friends to write in the book. Jimmy—who had always liked

Peggy Guggenheim's passport
photographs mounted in one of her
photo albums.
Private collection

Peggy's lack of pretentiousness and whom he had not seen for
many years—wrote fondly, "My love for you stretches from the
East River to the Grand Canal. It will last as long as both bodies
of water exist . . . and longer."[173] Just over two months later, on
December 23, Peggy, who had not been well for some time, died
in the hospital in Camposampiero, near Padua. That day in
Venice, there were floods, and Sindbad and Peggy Angela, both
knowing that this is what his mother would most appreciate,
were busy saving her legacy—her art collection, guest books, and
other possessions—from the tumultuous Venetian waters.

NOTES

Peggy Guggenheim's five guest books, kept during her years in residence at the Palazzo Venier dei Leoni, are referred to by page designations in which the first guest book is indicated by A, the second by B, the third by C, the fourth by D, and the fifth by E.

1. Peggy Guggenheim, *Out of This Century: Confessions of an Art Addict* (New York: Universe Books, 1979), p. 7.

2. Ibid.

3. Ibid., p. 49.

4. Quoted in Jacqueline Bograd Weld, *Peggy: The Wayward Guggenheim* (New York: E. P. Dutton, 1986), p. 16.

5. Edwin P. Hoyt, *The Guggenheims and the American Dream* (New York: Funk & Wagnalls, 1967), p. 218.

6. Guggenheim, *Out of This Century*, p. 10.

7. Ibid., p. 8.

8. Ibid., p. 18.

9. Although the years of Peggy's attendance at the Jacoby School are not totally certain, a photograph exists in which she and her class-mates are posed before a wall that has a banner with the year 1915 on it. The photograph is reproduced in Laurence Tacou-Rumney, *Peggy Guggenheim: A Collector's Album* (New York: Flammarion, 1996), trans. Ralph Rumney, p. 36.

10. Guggenheim, *Out of This Century*, p. 18.

11. Lucile Kohn to Virginia M. Dortch, May 25, 1973, in Virginia M. Dortch, ed., *Peggy Guggenheim and Her Friends* (Milan: Berenice Art Books, 1994), p. 37.

12. Guggenheim, *Out of This Century*, p. 18.

13. Kohn to Dortch, in Dortch, p. 37.

14. Guggenheim, *Out of This Century*, p. 22.

15. Ibid.

16. Ibid.

17. Ibid., p. 23.

18. Ibid.

19. Ibid., p. 27.

20. Joan Mellen, *Kay Boyle: Author of Herself* (New York: Farrar, Straus & Giroux, 1994), p. 133.

21. Guggenheim, *Out of This Century*, p. 33.

22. Mellen, p. 132.

23. Guggenheim, *Out of This Century*, p. 28.

24. Quoted in "Peggy Guggenheim: An Interview," in Dortch, pp. 9–10.

25. Guggenheim, *Out of This Century*, p. 55.

26. Ibid., p. 78.

27. Ibid., p. 79.

28. Ibid., p. 89.

29. Weld, p. 97, incorrectly attributes this appellation to Jane Bouché Strong, who would subsequently point out that "for a ten and a half year old going on eleven that would have been a bit much! . . . We all called it that." See Strong to Sindbad and Peggy Angela Vail, March 24, 1986, private collection.

30. Guggenheim, *Out of This Century*, p. 154.

31. Peggy Waldman to Peggy Guggenheim, May 11, 1937, quoted in Dortch, p. 54.

32. Guggenheim, *Out of This Century*, p. 161.

33. Ibid., p. 162.

34. Ibid.

35. Ibid., p. 163.

36. Quoted in ibid., p. 171.

37. Quoted in Joan M. Lukach, *Hilla Rebay: In Search of the Spirit in Art* (New York: George Braziller, 1983), p. 132.

38. Quoted in Weld, p. 146.

39. Guggenheim, *Out of This Century*, p. 180.

40. Ibid., p. 193.

41. Ibid., p. 194.

42. Weld, p. 446, cites *André Breton Presents Mexican Art* (June 5–22), an exhibition that was advertised for Art of This Century. However, there is no record of a checklist or a catalogue; nor are there any known reviews.

43. See farewell-party announcement reproduced in Angelica Zander Rudenstine, *The Peggy Guggenheim Collection, Venice* (New York: Harry N. Abrams, 1985), p. 758.

44. Guggenheim, *Out of This Century*, p. 197.

45. Herbert Read to Douglas Cooper, April 15, 1939, Getty Research Institute for the History of Art and the Humanities, Los Angeles, Special Collections, Douglas Cooper Papers.

46. Ibid.

47. Guggenheim, *Out of This Century*, p. 199.

48. Ibid., p. 204.

49. Ibid., p. 198.

50. Ibid., p. 216.

51. Ibid., p. 218.

52. Anthony Tommasini, *Virgil Thomson's Musical Portraits* (New York: Pendragon Press, 1996), p. 43.

53. Guggenheim, *Out of This Century*, p. 217.

54. Ibid., p. 209.

55. Ibid.

56. Rudenstine, p. 760.

57. Ibid.

58. Guggenheim, *Out of This Century*, p. 219.

59. André Breton to Peggy Guggenheim, August 13, 1965, private collection.

60. Guggenheim, *Out of This Century*, p. 245.

61. Jimmy Ernst, *A Not-So-Still Life* (New York: St. Martin's/Marek, 1984), pp. 199–200.

62. Ibid., p. 205.

63. Guggenheim, *Out of This Century*, pp. 250–51.

64. Ibid., p. 251.

65. Ibid., p. 258.

66. Ibid., p. 263.

67. Ibid., p. 270.

68. Rudenstine, p. 316.

69. Ibid., p. 763.

70. Leo Steinberg, telephone conversations with the author, November 1997.

71. Quoted in Weld, p. 273.

72. Peggy Guggenheim to Frederick J. Kiesler, March 4, 1942, reproduced in Rudenstine, p. 762.

73. Frederick J. Kiesler to Peggy Guggenheim, March 7, 1942, reproduced in ibid., p. 763.

74. Lisa Phillips, *Frederick Kiesler* (New York: Whitney Museum of American Art in association with W. W. Norton & Company, 1989), p. 114.

75. Frederick J. Kiesler, untitled typescript, 1942, in the library of the Peggy Guggenheim Collection, p. 1.

76. Frederick J. Kiesler, "Note on Designing the Gallery," 1942, typescript in the library of the Peggy Guggenheim Collection, p. 1.

77. Guggenheim, *Out of This Century*, p. 274.

78. Weld, p. 288.

79. Kiesler, untitled typescript, p. 2.

80. Guggenheim, *Out of This Century*, pp. 275–76.

81. Quoted in Weld, p. 301.

82. Clement Greenberg, review in *The Nation*, December 26, 1942, quoted in *Laurence Vail*, exh. cat. (New York: Noah Goldowsky, 1974), unpaginated.

83. Guggenheim, *Out of This Century*, p. 280.

84. Jeffrey Potter, *To a Violent Grave: An Oral Biography of Jackson Pollock* (New York: G. P. Putnam's Sons, 1985), p. 71.

85. Clement Greenberg, review in *The Nation*, May 29, 1943, quoted in Rudenstine, p. 774.

86. Guggenheim, *Out of This Century*, p. 315.

87. Robert Motherwell, review in *Partisan Review* (winter 1944), quoted in Rudenstine, p. 776.

88. Nell Blaine to Virginia M. Dortch, June 14, 1977, in Dortch, p. 123.

89. Weld, p. 313.

90. Rudenstine, p. 777.

91. Clement Greenberg, review in *The Nation*, April 7, 1944, quoted in ibid., p. 784.

92. Peggy Guggenheim to David Porter, November 17, [1943 or 1945], Archives of American Art, Smithsonian Institution, David Porter Papers. This letter is not dated with a year, but it relates to one of two exhibitions at Art of This Century: *Exhibition by 31 Women*, held in 1943, or *The Women*, held in 1945.

93. Clyfford Still to Virginia M. Dortch, October 14, 1971, in Dortch, p. 122.

94. Clement Greenberg, review in *The Nation*, April 13, 1946, quoted in Rudenstine, p. 791.

95. Guggenheim, *Out of This Century*, p. 322.

96. Herbert Read to Peggy Guggenheim, March 28, 1946, private collection.

97. Djuna Barnes to Peggy Guggenheim, November 9, 1960, private collection.

98. Guggenheim, *Out of This Century*, p. 324.

99. Ibid., p. 320.

100. Quoted in Weld, p. 353.

101. The phrase appears on the righthand catalogue page; reproduced in Rudenstine, p. 792.

102. Greenberg, review in *The Nation*, February 1, 1947, quoted in ibid., p. 794.

103. Greenberg, review in *The Nation*, May 31, 1947, quoted in ibid., p. 798.

104. Guggenheim, *Out of This Century*, p. 329.

105. Ibid.

106. Ibid.

107. Ibid.

108. Lee Miller, "Venice Biennale," British *Vogue* (August 1948), p. 90.

109. Guggenheim, *Out of This Century*, p. 329.

110. Vittorio Carrain to Dortch, March 10, 1972 and April 11, 1983, in Dortch, p. 150.

111. Guggenheim, *Out of This Century*, p. 341.

112. A7 right.

113. Guggenheim, *Out of This Century*, p. 334.

114. A20 left.

115. Guggenheim, *Out of This Century*, p. 346.

116. Sam Hunter, telephone conversation with the author, August 1997.

117. A27.

118. A43 left.

119. Guggenheim, *Out of This Century*, p. 336.

120. Quoted in Weld, p. 373.

121. Guggenheim, *Out of This Century*, p. 338.

122. A73 right.

123. A77 right.

124. Ibid.

125. B9 right.

126. B11 left.

127. B13 right.

128. Eugene Kolb, preface to *Abstract and Surrealist Paintings*, exh. cat. (Tel Aviv: Tel-Aviv Museum, 1955), unpaginated.

129. B53 right.

130. B59 left.

131. B75 right.

132. Guggenheim, *Out of This Century*, p. 341.

133. Ibid.

134. B84 left.

135. B83 left.

136. Ned Rorem to the author, May 19, 1997.

137. Helen Frankenthaler to the author, October 10, 1997.

138. B98 right.

139. Some people considered Gregorich a man of questionable character, but he apparently had a genuine affection for Peggy. See Weld, pp. 378–81.

140. Guggenheim, *Out of This Century*, p. 351.

141. Peggy Guggenheim, introduction to *Edmondo Bacci*, exh. cat. (Milan: Il Naviglio, 1957), unpaginated.

142. C4 left.

143. Buffie Johnson, interview with the author, New York, May 11, 1997.

144. Giovanni Carandente to Virginia M. Dortch, January 2, 1984, in Dortch, p. 161.

145. C22 left.

146. C69 left.

147. Leo Steinberg, telephone conversations with the author, November 1997.

148. Ibid.

149. Allen Ginsberg to Peggy Guggenheim, July 25, 1957, private collection.

150. C82 left and right.

151. C88 right.

152. James Lord, *Picasso and Dora* (New York: Farrar, Straus & Giroux, 1995), p. 309.

153. Guggenheim, *Out of This Century*, p. 361.

154. Ibid., p. 363.

155. Ibid., p. 364.

156. Peggy Guggenheim to Robert Brady, July 6, 1960, Robert Brady Foundation, Cuernavaca.

157. C140 left.

158. C142 left and right.

159. Bryan Robertson, "A Face-Lift for Guggenheim," *The Spectator*, June 13, 1981, p. 23.

160. Guggenheim, *Out of This Century*, p. 379.

161. D35 left.

162. D35 right.

163. D77 right.

164. D78 left.

165. Seamus Heaney to the author, March 14, 1997.

166. Quoted in Weld, p. 397.

167. D153 right.

168. E32 right.

169. Guggenheim, *Out of This Century*, p. 374.

170. Ibid.

171. Gore Vidal to Virginia M. Dortch, April 23, 1983, quoted in Dortch, p. 149.

172. E84 left.

173. E87 left.

The History of a Courtship

Thomas M. Messer

I first met Peggy Guggenheim in the fall of 1956, not long after I resigned the directorship of the American Federation of Arts in New York to take charge of the Institute of Contemporary Art in Boston. My wife, Remi, and I were in Venice at the end of a summer vacation in Europe. Slim and dark-haired, Peggy received us agreeably—though her manner even then was poised on the border between engagingly direct and brusque—at her home, the Palazzo Venier dei Leoni. She was interested in my going to Boston and wanted to know how I was going to work out with Perry Rathbone, the director of the Museum of Fine Arts. Since the relationship between the museum and the institute was at the time being redefined, this delicate question was on everyone's mind, but only Peggy would broach it so bluntly.

Peggy showed us paintings by Edmondo Bacci and Tancredi, artists she was promoting at the time. She offered us a handsome Bacci painting for our private collection at three hundred dollars. After some verbal skirmishes, she shamed me into buying it, and it would serve as a souvenir of my first encounter with the "ultima Dogaressa," as some Venetians called her. Decades later, after Peggy's death, I gave the painting to the Guggenheim for the Peggy Guggenheim Collection.

In any case, it was not until a few years after my appointment to the directorship of the Solomon R. Guggenheim Museum in 1961 that my contact with Peggy became regularized. It was in this year too that coming to terms with her regarding the disposition of her collection was for the first time discussed with Harry F. Guggenheim, then president of the Solomon R. Guggenheim Foundation. Harry was Solomon's nephew and Peggy's cousin. Judging from a letter of September 10, 1961, written to the foundation's counsel, Chauncey Newlin, Peggy did not favor us: "The best place for the pictures after my death

Marc Chagall
Rain (La Pluie), 1911
Oil (and charcoal?) on canvas,
86.7 x 108 cm
Peggy Guggenheim Collection
76.2553 PG 63

would be the Modern Museum [Galleria Internazionale d'Arte Moderna di Ca' Pesaro] of Venice." But something must have occurred to modify her thinking over the next few years, for on August 4, 1964, Harry wrote to Peggy in response to "your inquiry concerning the possibility of the Solomon R. Guggenheim Foundation ultimately taking over the administration of your gallery in Venice and operating it." Peggy responded on August 26, "I am very happy that you have not excluded my idea as an eventual possibility."

Typically, however, Peggy had second thoughts. Less than a year later, on March 8, 1965, she admitted to Harry, "I never wrote to you again about my eventual leaving the collection to your Museum, as I was a little afraid of being swallowed up by your much more important Foundation." Ever the gentleman and also never one to lose face, Harry replied on March 12, "As for your collection eventually coming to our Museum here in New York, I had really never given any thought to it. . . . I have no idea what your problems or wishes are."

For some time thereafter, any idea of pursuing the final disposition of Peggy's collection was dropped in favor of a more limited project, the organization of a selection of works from her collection to be exhibited at the Guggenheim Museum in New York. Though this exhibition had appeal in and of itself, it was from its inception implicitly linked to hopes of obtaining Peggy's collection. In her letter of March 8, she also wrote, "Thank you so much for your kind invitation to show my collection at the Guggenheim Museum," but then mentioned the problems and resulting fatigue she had experienced in connection with an exhibition of her collection at the Tate Gallery, London, which was held from December 1964 to March 1965. Harry, addressing himself to this matter in his letter of March 12, responded, "I can understand how you feel about another exhibition of your pictures right now, following all the trouble and work at the Tate exhibition. . . . when you are ready to talk about it . . . arrangements will be facilitated and made quite easy for you by Tom Messer, our Director."

Harry, probably upon my urging, did not leave it at that. "How would you feel," he wrote on December 16, "about a Guggenheim Jeune long summer show at the Guggenheim in New York in 1967?" (Harry referred to "Guggenheim Jeune" in homage to the London gallery she ran during 1938–39.) Peggy responded on January 1, 1966, "I'm afraid that the only time I can let the Collection leave Venice is between November and Easter when my Museum is closed." In my very first letter addressed to Peggy in that same month, I assured her that "nothing would please me more than to carry out such a project." When, subsequently, I informed her that "I plan to be in Venice from June 25 for the rest of the month," I therewith announced the first of a dozen or so pilgrimages I was to make to Peggy's palazzo during her lifetime. Peggy did not immediately react to my announcement, and when we met, she kept her distance from me. Apart from her persisting fears about being "swallowed up" by the foundation in New York, her relationship with the Guggenheim family was far from close as a result of a longstanding antagonism between her and Hilla Rebay, uncle Solomon's "muse" and the Guggenheim's first director. Knowing this, I had reason to suspect that she saw me as Harry's agent—as an agent of the Guggenheims—and as someone toward whom a posture of caution was in order.

During our early acquaintance, Peggy left the burden of approach entirely to me. I would buy huge bouquets of flowers and when the intercom voice at the palazzo gate intoned its "*pronto*," I would, flowers in hand, use one of the few Italian

words then at my command to reply *"fiori."* It worked, and
Peggy, to whom I eventually told the story, liked it and became
more readily accessible. But even long after we had established a
friendlier relationship, Peggy would lapse into moods of suspi-
ciousness and wariness.

The courtship, however, continued. Upon my return from
Italy, Harry wrote to Peggy rather optimistically on August 9,
"We are all happy to know that at long last, come 1968, we shall
have an exhibition of Guggenheim Jeune at the Guggenheim."
On September 24, she responded guardedly, "I did indeed talk to
Tom Messer . . . and we agreed to decide next spring when I
could be ready to have another exhibition."

A few months later, in a letter addressed to me on January 11,
1967, she put her commitment in writing, thereby creating
something of a panic in our ranks by stating, "I think it would be
advisable to have the show with you next winter." We had
intended that the exhibition be held in late 1968, and holding
the exhibition in the winter of 1967–68 would have required the
rescheduling of exhibitions to which we were already committed.
Not wishing to appear negative, however, I responded on
January 18 that "if you confirm the 1967–68 winter booking
finally and irrevocably, I shall move the necessary mountains to
accommodate it." With less circumspection, Harry wrote to her
on January 23, "We are delighted that you have decided to send
your collection earlier than anticipated." To which Peggy
responded on January 29, "I am pleased to know that everything
will be alright for 1967."

Such relatively auspicious beginnings were brought to a
standstill as a result of the tragic death of Peggy's daughter,
Pegeen Vail, on March 1. There is no question that this loss
proved a body blow from which, in a sense, Peggy never fully
recovered. Exhibition plans obviously had to be shelved, and it
was not until April 5 that I deemed it appropriate to address the
business at hand. "Quite understandably," I wrote, "I have not
heard from you recently. . . . I find that I could adjust previous
plans to arrange for a showing early December 1967 into early
February 1968."

Through no fault of Peggy's, my initial doubts regarding
the feasibility of the proposed dates proved well-founded.
In a letter of April 11, the first communication I had following
Pegeen's death, Peggy wrote, "It is most unfortunate that I
asked you to change the date of the exhibition of my collection
in the Guggenheim Museum to 1967. . . . I will be in mourning

for a year and could not possibly consider any parties or doing any publicity myself this year." I must have concluded well before Peggy's response that delays would be unavoidable, for I replied on April 19, "I had not made the change from 1968 to 1967 final, since it would have involved us in a great deal of difficult reorganization."

Then, during a summer visit with Peggy, exhibition plans were discussed in some detail and lists were drawn up. The show was rescheduled to open in January 1969. I was thus able to review the exhibition's status in writing, concluding in a vein indicative of some tenseness in our conversations: "I thoroughly enjoyed my visit with you, much appreciated your candor, and hope you didn't mind mine."

During her depression as a result of Pegeen's death, Peggy was not easy to deal with. Following my summer visit, she had written to me in evident ill humor: "I am feeling so completely unfit to face the public that I can't bear to think of coming to New York next year and get into a whirl of parties and press reviews." For good measure, she added, "I do not like your list. It almost looks as though I had stopped collecting after Pollock. Also your values are much too low." In self-defense, I wrote back on November 30, "With regard to the list, it should certainly reflect correctly your collecting personality. . . . My insurance list was no more than a personal evaluation made upon your request." This capitulation notwithstanding, Peggy returned to the same matter on April 11, 1968, with more emphasis: "I have been speaking to several people about your selection from my collection and have come to the conclusion that it is not at all fair to leave out so many important works as it gives a very bad idea of my collection. Therefore I must insist that you include the following works or give up the show altogether." Thoroughly cowed by such threats I responded on April 18, "Of course we do not even want to think about giving up a show to which we are all deeply committed. The additions which you have indicated are eminently acceptable and will, I feel sure, enrich the situation."

Peggy's moods and humors, whether good or bad, rarely remained the same for any length of time, but the year following Pegeen's death as a whole reflected her discouragement more than her positive outlook. In a letter of July 12, following one of my visits, she made appreciative mention of "your beautiful flowers" and even returned to the issue of her collection's eventual disposition for the first time since 1965. But what she had to say

failed to hold out much hope: "I did not tell you," she wrote, "but I am leaving the house and the collection here, and Italy has not lost it after all. It is not that I think that they deserve it, but the thing is complete in itself and must remain so."

Meanwhile, the arrangements for the exhibition in New York were moving along. Peggy discussed details in the same letter as well as in a subsequent one of July 17, informing me that "Sattis [a Venetian fine-arts shipping company] came this morning to measure so no more changes will be considered," and "I have rewritten my introduction starting from the fifth paragraph before the end of the Tate Gallery text." On the other hand, still nervous about dates and possible complications in my scheduling, I wrote apprehensively as late as September 6, "Let me confirm that the opening date for the exhibition is now irrevocably set for January 15, 1969."

Then, out of the clear blue sky, came another outburst for which I was ill prepared. On September 6, the same day I was writing to her, she hurled the following accusation at me: "I have received an invitation to your Peruvian show [*Mastercraftsmen of Ancient Peru*, an exhibition held October 1968–January 1969] and now realize why you have put off my show until January. I imagine it has something to do with Guggenheim interests in South America. . . . I feel very badly about this as you can imagine." And proceeding in the same combative vein, Peggy demanded, "I would like first of all a guaranty from you about how many paintings you will restore for me. . . . The only reason I lend my collection is to get it restored." Since I had had occasion to complain in the past that so many of our warmly amicable visits tended to be followed up by nasty letters from her, Peggy felt moved to remark, "I suppose you will consider this another nasty letter. I hope not." In my response of September 10, I allowed that "after talking to you at length during the summer I can no longer think of your letters as nasty, but I do think that you are jumping to false conclusions." I then explained truthfully that "the Peruvian show has nothing, whatsoever, to do with what you assume."

But the storm passed as suddenly as it had gathered, and for a while at least, all proceeded rather serenely and in low key. "Thank you very much for your nice telegram. No, there was no cause for alarm," wrote Peggy on November 6, when I expressed concern about reports of floods in Venice. On December 2, I replied, "I am happy to hear that the aqua was not so alta." Then, with lingering unease, I added, "The great opening is

FACING PAGE

Gino Severini
Sea=Dancer (Mare=Ballerina),
January 1914
Oil on canvas, 105.3 x 85.9 cm,
including artist's painted frame
Peggy Guggenheim Collection
76.2553 PG 32

133

scheduled for January 15." Before this, on November 14, Peggy had acknowledged, "I have just received the introductions of the catalogue for my exhibition. I am extremely pleased with them." She then added, "I am sending a [Theo] van Doesburg after all . . . as it is badly in need of repair. . . . Also, the [Giuseppe] Santomaso which you included in your original list, and which I removed but which I now deem necessary to show (if not too late) as he has become a Trustee of the [Peggy Guggenheim] Foundation."

On December 13, I wrote with obvious relief, "We have now completed a detailed check of the shipment from Venice and . . . trivia apart, everything is in good order." On December 17, Peggy let me know, "I would like to stay in a small hotel near the Museum. What about the Adams?" But the suggestion was withdrawn on December 22 because "I have been told by a friend that the Adams Hotel is HORRIBLE." Also, since I had written before that I was suffering from the Hong Kong flu, she now asked, "Could you please, if possible, arrange to have your doctor give me an anti–Hong Kong flu injection. But most of all I want to know how long I am to be Harry's guest." I was at this time away from New York, and these questions were fully answered by my secretary in a letter dated December 26.

There was no further correspondence prior to Peggy's arrival in New York on the day before the grand opening of our exhibition, *Works from the Peggy Guggenheim Foundation*, on January 15, 1969. It was, in keeping with the season, a cold winter afternoon. Robin Green, the museum's public affairs offi- cer, accompanied me in a limousine to JFK airport at around three p.m. We waited for a long time, but Peggy had failed to appear. Milling around dejectedly in the crowded arrival area, I suddenly spied her, and we fell into each other's arms—I out of relief; she because her entire baggage was lost, and she needed help. We had naturally provided for first-class passage, but Peggy, as parsimonious with other people's money as with her own, insisted upon traveling economy class. Fussy and difficult though she could be at times, she was unperturbed and only mildly annoyed that her evening toilette was evidently heading toward some distant continent. Our offers to take her shopping were gratefully but firmly rejected. She said that she would come to the black-tie opening "in her boots," which is exactly what she did and with considerable panache.

A small family dinner had been planned for the evening of Peggy's arrival. Peter Lawson-Johnston, Solomon's grandson and

at the time vice president of our foundation, presided in Harry's
absence, which was due to the latter's illness. It was the first
occasion for her to see my installation of her collection at the
Guggenheim. Such moments are always uneasy, but particularly
with a person as moody and unpredictable as Peggy. She walked
into the museum with me before the arrival of other guests, took
a long and thoughtful look, and made two pronouncements:
"My pictures now look like postage stamps," and "If my uncle
Solomon can now see me, he is surely turning in his grave."
Such asides notwithstanding, Peggy was, during her first public
evening, as well as the grand opening the following night,
pleased and gracious, masterful in impromptu press encounters,
and delighted with the many friends who turned out to see her.
Apart from showing signs of a more or less permanent streak of
sadness—surely deepened by the memory of Pegeen's death—she
was cheerful and delightful throughout her New York stay.

The most far-reaching effect of Peggy's visit was her decision,
long in gestation no doubt, to leave her collection in the care of
the Solomon R. Guggenheim Foundation. This decision was

something she communicated to me and which, in turn, I was able to convey to Harry, who, sad to remember, remained incapacitated throughout her visit and was therefore unable to see her. Though uncertain and vacillating when details, arrangements, and procedures were at issue, Peggy held firm to her gift commitment once it was made. A contractual letter stating the conditions of legal transfers from Peggy Guggenheim to the Peggy Guggenheim Foundation, and then from that entity to the Solomon R. Guggenheim Foundation, was duly submitted on January 27. This was followed, on February 14, by my proposals to embark upon a program of conservation for her collection under Guggenheim Museum auspices and by Harry's offer to her of a life membership.

My summer visit to Peggy's palazzo was so friendly that upon returning from Europe, I wrote on August 21, "I felt toward you more than ever, open and relaxed, protective and affectionate." I also reported on my visit to Romania and related efforts to secure important Constantin Brancusi sculptures for a retrospective exhibition, which we were to share with the Art Institute of Chicago and the Philadelphia Museum of Art; the

Pablo Picasso
On the Beach (*La Baignade*),
February 12, 1937
Oil, conté crayon, and chalk on canvas,
129.1 x 194 cm
Peggy Guggenheim Collection
76.2553 PG 5

FACING PAGE

El Lissitzky
Untitled, ca. 1919–20
Oil on canvas, 79.6 x 49.6 cm
Peggy Guggenheim Collection
76.2553 PG 43

Guggenheim Museum showing was to open in November. I had my eye on the two Brancusis in her collection: *Maiastra* (1912 [?]) and *Bird in Space* (*L'Oiseau dans l'espace*, 1932–40). "I got more glamorous Brancusis, but no birds to speak of from anyone, except from you, if you were angelically disposed, as I hope you will be," I wrote. She was not and a brief angelic phase was waning again. On October 1, she wrote that "the last five paintings came back [from New York] at last. . . . Four are fine, but the Cubist Picasso [*The Poet* (*Le Poète*, August 1911)] looks like hell."

Before I could answer her charge leveled at the first stages of a mutually agreed conservation program that had resulted in a competent cleaning of *The Poet*'s canvas surface, she continued on October 3, "Was particularly upset yesterday when I again put my mind on the Picasso painting of the poet." Then, switching subjects, "I am still trying to transfer this house to you with the least expense. That is without paying taxes and if possible without paying a lawyer." On October 17, I had a chance to return to the Picasso issue and wrote that "our conservation people would really like you to send back the Picasso together with anything else in need of conservation." And hoping against hope, I returned once again to our upcoming Brancusi exhibition: "I wonder whether I may approach you now with a formal request for your two Brancusis." The matter was finally put to rest by Peggy's reply of November 30: "Sorry but I did not feel like sending my two pieces but the less travel the better." She also informed me that "I have now decided not to send back any paintings to America [for conservation]."

On January 2, 1970, she wrote, to the obvious discomfort of our conservation experts, "I have not yet decided what to do with *The Poet*. Everyone gives me different advice but I think a new coat of varnish will be the best solution." Finally, in the same letter, she stated, "I am trying now to put this house in the name of the Solomon Guggenheim Museum so as not to have to make two transfers." Otherwise, partly perhaps because the urgencies imposed by the exhibition *Works from the Peggy Guggenheim Foundation* were no longer upon us, correspondence between us became less frequent. After another summer visit to Venice, which was characteristically amicable, I had occasion to write to Peggy on August 21, "As always, visiting with you and talking to you was rewarding and heart-warming."

The following year, 1971, provided a new and not at all pleasant subject for our correspondence. My first inkling of the

FACING PAGE

Joan Miró
Seated Woman II (Femme assise II),
February 27, 1939
Oil on canvas, 162 x 130 cm
Peggy Guggenheim Collection
76.2553 PG 93

crisis came through a letter, dated February 10, Peggy wrote to her lawyer-accountant, Bernard Reis, which he forwarded to me: "I had a bad surprise while I was in London; the girls [her servants] phoned to say that thieves had broken into my house and stolen 13 paintings." The circumstances of the theft were never particularly clear to me, nor were those of their speedy recovery. It was all *molto Italiano*, with the chief of police emerging as the hero. I cabled Peggy on February 22: "SO VERY RELIEVED." And followed up on February 25: "Would you want me to send Orrin Riley, our conservator in chief, to see how your security setup can be improved? Would you also let me know whether the damage reported in the case of one work needs our attention?" By way of reply, I received a letter, dated March 14, which clearly was not written by Peggy, except for the few corrections inscribed upon the typed text in her handwriting. The somewhat ponderous contents—articulated no doubt by Peggy's assistant, John Hohnsbeen—proposed with respect to the security system that "I would be most grateful if the Guggenheim Museum could help defray this expense." Then, in Peggy's handwriting: "Or should I possibly get it off my income tax?" I traveled to Venice to survey the damage and assess our future options. I found Peggy in high spirits, and we spent perhaps the most uninhibited and lovely time together, ever. She confirmed my own sentiments by writing to me on September 3, "We had such a nice, gay evening the other night before you left. I was very grateful because such evenings are very rare nowadays. Love."

Peggy could be—and often was—simultaneously generous and stingy, merry and sad, outgoing and withdrawn, simple and complex. She was obsessively preoccupied with material things, yet not unconcerned with principle (although the nature of her morality was quirky and often difficult to establish). She had a warm and authentic relationship toward art and artists, but her collecting taste was never methodic and often not even attentive. She was neither a scholar nor an intellectual, although she appreciated and admired the company of both and moved within such circles with ease and tact. She was nothing if not direct and outspoken, yet her straightforwardness—which incidentally is a Guggenheim trait—consciously or otherwise, masked greater complexities of which she may or may not have been aware. Above all, there was something indescribably sad, even tragic, about Peggy. To my mind, the strokes of fate that she suffered did not fully account for this. In some strange way, she seemed troubled about her very existence, and her tendency

to surround herself with men and women of quality was rooted perhaps in her need for attachments that would uphold her. Despite such constraints, Peggy was capable of great courage, style, and grandeur, and she translated these attributes into an admirable life.

Peggy remained as mercurial as ever, and she broke my heart by writing on November 11, "No one came to see about the restoration of the pictures or to see about security measures. Does that mean that the Guggenheim Museum has given up the project? . . . It seems ages since our gay dinner at the Angelo." I had to tell her on November 30: "You are jumping to conclusions . . . . Orrin Riley's trip was postponed for unrelated reasons and he is scheduled now to be in Venice [in January 1972]." But a final blow came in another letter from Peggy, this one simply dated December: "I am very sorry to have to tell you that January is too late. Why did you put it off so long? Last night thieves came, broke through the grills of the sitting-room window and carried off . . . 17 [paintings] in all." The second such calamity within one year left me feeling stoic rather than upset—at least in part because one began to expect a repetition of the pattern surrounding the previous theft. Indeed, subsequent events bore out my instincts; almost immediately, the works were recovered.

Before the resumption of my correspondence with Peggy after a period of several months, Peter Lawson-Johnston—who had become president of the Solomon R. Guggenheim Foundation in 1969—had grown concerned about Peggy's request for financial aid and had written to her on February 29, 1972, "It has come to my attention that you may be prepared to sell a work of art from your collection to raise the necessary funds [for the security system]. If so, would you consider selling it to us?" Somewhat to my surprise, Peggy responded quickly to Peter on March 8, "I think your suggestion of buying a picture from my collection is acceptable. The details can be worked out with Messer." Trying to keep the subject alive, I wrote on April 10 that "Peter Lawson-Johnston has told me of your recent letter and I am delighted to know that his proposal to you is acceptable."

The garden of the Peggy Guggenheim Collection, photographed in 1998 by Sergio Martucci.

FACING PAGE

Alberto Giacometti
Standing Woman ("Leoni") (*Femme debout ["Leoni"]*), 1947 (cast November 1957)
Bronze, 153 cm high, including base
Peggy Guggenheim Collection
76.2553 PG 134

142

My visit to Venice in early 1973 took place in a climate nothing less than euphoric—"Dear Tom nice Tom sweet Tom," Peggy wrote in February, no doubt in further allusion to my complaints about her nasty epistolary manners. "Do come around the middle of the month. If you wish I can put you up. Love"— and she seemed entirely willing to pay for the already installed security system with funds derived from our payment for a work of art that would formally leave Peggy's collection to become part of the Guggenheim Museum's permanent collection in New York. After my return to New York, I wrote on April 17 that "my half-day visit with you remains unforgettable" and touched upon a number of pending issues, among them to consummate the transfer, in keeping with our agreed bargain, of Joseph Cornell's *Fortune Telling Parrot (Parrot Music Box)* (ca. 1937–38) to the Guggenheim Museum in New York. In a subsequent letter, Peggy started with the same affectionate appellation as in February, only to continue, "As to the Cornell, I have decided not to let it go to the Guggenheim Museum." Nor did she offer to let anything else take its place. There was nothing for me to do but respond gently and lovingly on June 19, "As ever, I find it easy enough to agree with your changing propositions." It should be added in connection with the subject of the security system that, throughout Peggy's lifetime, it remained largely ineffective despite our best efforts. She either forgot to turn it on or, having done so, failed to follow procedures that would control it as she reentered the palazzo. The effect of such negligence was that the police station wished the system had never been installed; in an attempt to save face by pretending that she was merely testing, Peggy always greeted the onrushing *polizia* with *"prova, prova!"*

Despite continued efforts by White & Case, our legal representatives, and Graziadei, the charmingly named Italian law firm charged with the same matter in Italy, excruciatingly slow progress was being made on the legal front with efforts to have arrangements between the Peggy Guggenheim Foundation and the Solomon R. Guggenheim Foundation ratified by the Italian authorities. Peter, toward whom Peggy had developed warm sympathies, had written to her on July 25, 1972, in a spirit as yet untainted by skepticism: "I gather everything will be wound up relatively soon regarding our formal acceptance of your gift of Palazzo Venier dei Leoni."

In 1973, things were progressing satisfactorily, with the exception of an idea of Peggy's that caused me some concern. In

Marino Marini
The Angel of the City (*L'angelo della città*),
1948 (cast 1950?)
Bronze, 247.9 x 106 cm, including base
Peggy Guggenheim Collection
76.2553 PG 183

conversations with me, she introduced the notion that her favorite grandson, Nicolas Hélion, should become "curator" of her collection after her death. While I remained noncommittal, Nicolas wrote in an undated letter in 1973, "Ma grand-mère, Madame Peggy Guggenheim, vous a entretenu de mon project qui est de devenir directeur de la fondation de Venise." (My grandmother, Madame Peggy Guggenheim, has spoken to you of my desire to become director of the Venice museum.) He proceeded to questions as to his salary if he came to the New York museum prior to such an assignment. After clarifying the distinction between a trainee and a salaried position, I answered on July 19, "I have suggested . . . that if in future you were to take an active part, you would have to be properly prepared and qualified." I made arrangements for his university enrollment, but it became clear in the meantime that Nicolas had developed other interests, and the matter was gradually dropped. Apart from an unsuccessful loan request in November—this time for a work by Alberto Giacometti in Peggy's collection—1973 continued to be relatively calm.

On January 2, 1974, I wrote to Peggy, "We mused about the possibility of my return visit to Venice . . . and if so, whether you would have me . . . in February?" Whereupon, Peggy responded by telling me about "a dog who got the mange, then broke his foot, and on top of all, I got arthritis" and then adding "but, if you want to come so please do." Apparently, I could not resist the warmth of this invitation, and there were also new legal developments for which we needed Peggy's approvals.

Sometime after my return, I wrote on April 22, "It appears that the transfer of the Palazzo has indeed been completed" and on October 21, Peter confirmed it in a letter to Peggy, "I have just been informed about the legal arrangements regarding your collection." So far so good, but then she replied on November 1, "There is another problem. The place is a shambles as all the rain comes in and is beginning to ruin all the pictures." Peggy's revelations unfortunately were neither exaggerated nor unexpected, and for some time the decision to accept her gift remained an issue among the foundation's trustees, many of whom doubted the prudence of accepting an unendowed palazzo and collection—no matter how valuable. Luckily for those who argued differently, things had reached a point of no return, and those favoring acceptance included Peter, the foundation's president. The trustees' authorizing documents were thus signed with some vestigial reluctance. Many years of negotiations were about to be finalized, and the issue of providing financial assistance for the maintenance of the palazzo and the collection was much discussed. Relative to it, in a memorandum from me to Peter, I suggested that "we accept responsibility in principle but that we ourselves be involved in the remedy." In accordance with this line of reasoning, Peter wrote to Peggy on December 2, "I believe that the Board [of trustees] will approve of emergency expenditures for essential restoration [and] renovation under certain conditions."

The Peggy Guggenheim Foundation minutes approving the transfer of the collection and palazzo from it to the Solomon R. Guggenheim Foundation were dated July 17, 1975, but uncertainty about the terms, as well as certain procedural aspects, continued to bother both sides. On August 22, I worried about the artworks, writing to Peggy, "The matter of the conditions of some works remains a very grave concern and I wonder whether you would receive Orrin Riley if I dispatched him to Venice." The answer this time came from Hohnsbeen, and although Peggy wished what she had to say to come to me by indirection, the letter itself is filled with her inimitable touches. Hohnsbeen may have written that "it is, of course, important that Orrin Riley be given as much time as possible to inspect the collection," but this is followed in Peggy's suspicious vein: "She [Peggy] was most

Palazzo Venier dei Leoni, after 1979.

upset to learn that you wished the conditions she made with
Harry Guggenheim withdrawn, and she insisted they be rein-
stated. Why do you want this left out?" In the absence of any
basis whatsoever for such a charge, I decided not to bother with
Hohnsbeen but to wire directly to Peggy on September 12, "What
you assume to be a withdrawal of your conditions you need not
fear, Peggy. No one here has any thought, let alone intention, to
change our agreement." Peggy remained unconvinced, writing to
me on November 14, "Bernard [Reis] told me that I should have
a letter from you, so I am afraid I cannot accept your cable as a
guarantee."

As so often in the past, such storms—engendered by Peggy
on the basis of hearsay or misunderstood information—passed,
and good weather stayed until the next downpour. In 1976, the
Peggy Guggenheim Foundation was finally terminated, and legal
possession of the collection and palazzo was transferred to the
Solomon R. Guggenheim Foundation.

After I wrote to Peggy on May 17, 1976, that "the Biennale
calamity is upon us and since I have some official contact with it
this time, I will not be able to avoid Venice in July," she
received me in May with her usual warmth and cordiality. It was
never difficult for me to establish contact with her in face-to-face
meetings. She would sit me down in her living room, give me a
drink, and immediately and unhesitatingly ask me questions
that others might have put with some hesitation if at all.
Conventional inquiries were used for warming-up purposes only.
After this, she wanted to know details about her New York rela-
tives, specifically about how I got along with my Guggenheims.
I told her stories about how difficult and virtually impossible it
used to be to say "no" to Harry during his lifetime (he had died
in 1971); the best I could ever do was to say, "Yes sir, but . . . ."
She responded, "I love that, what you said was 'Yes, but no!'"
Looking at me with smiling inquisitiveness, she would ask
whether I had any girlfriends, and what my wife's attitude was
in such situations. My opinion about the sexual preferences
of common acquaintances was regularly sought, and any indis-
cretion that I was willing to traffic was received with childlike
gratitude.

My interactions with Peggy during visits to Venice were
pleasant interludes, but back in New York more substantial
issues were never far away. Not long after my return from my
visit in May, we had a new problem, as a letter of mine, dated
July 26, proved. I wrote to Peggy about a Fernand Léger paint-

ing—one of his *Contrastes de formes*—that now appeared to be of uncertain authorship. I was obliged to tell her that it would probably not figure in future publications of the Peggy Guggenheim Collection. For some time following the disclosure Peggy clung to "her favorite painting." But on October 18, she tempered such hopes with an admirable touch of realism: "I have left a letter," Peggy writes on that date, "giving you the authority to dispose of the Léger." But it took many reminders before, only two months prior to her death, she handed me a typed slip made up of two unequivocal statements that by strict logic would be considered mutually exclusive. The first sentence read: "I hereby authorize Thomas Messer to dispose of by sale or exchange CON-TRASTE DE FORMES by FERNAND LEGER dated 1913 if it should be advisable." To which, however, she added: "Also insist that anything I will to the Guggenheim Museum can never be sold."

In the late 1970s, Peggy often thought and spoke of her death, probably because of her deteriorating physical condition, especially the intensification of her arthritis, and the pain connected with it, which never left her. But there was neither self-pity nor lament as her life moved toward its close. Among the questions she posed were those concerning arrangements regarding the palazzo. She was apprehensive that anyone might stay there after her death, and I assured her that this was not part of our thinking. For obvious reasons, I did not as a rule volunteer intentions, but when she "supposed" that we might transform the entire palazzo into gallery spaces, I nodded agreement. She remained concerned with material matters to the end, writing to me on May 18, 1977, "As I had to pay this tax in the name of the Solomon Guggenheim I think it is only right that I should be reimbursed." As usual in such situations, I answered meekly, "We shall be glad to reimburse you for the tax which you have paid out."

A year later, on June 1, 1978, Peggy wrote to Peter, "I have asked the American consul to come here from Trieste to make a power of attorney for Sindbad [her son]. . . . I think everything is covered." Still concerned with possessions, Peggy apparently asked Hohnsbeen to write to Angelica Zander Rudenstine, to whom I had assigned the catalogue research for the Peggy Guggenheim Collection: "I would like to leave the dining-room furniture to the Solomon R. Guggenheim, but I will only leave it to them on the condition that it remains in the dining room here as a permanent part of the collection never to be sold." To allay her concerns, I wrote on January 4, 1979, "I took the matter to the Board and enclose the pertinent passage as well as the resolution which, I trust, is in keeping with your request."

On April 16 followed my periodic announcement of a forthcoming visit: "I am scheduled to participate in Venice Biennale meetings on May 3, 4, and 5. I would love to see you and will call upon arrival." The visit took place as indicated despite her ailments and, I believe, her growing presentiments of death. Peggy was cheerful and lovely. Her flock of dogs was reduced by attrition to two, and we joked that my longstanding promise to hurry to Venice immediately upon her demise to take care of the dogs was now a much less extensive chore. As it turned out, I never had to fulfill this pledge at all, since the last of her "beloved babies" (as she called her canine brood) died, with considerable tact and finesse, a few days before his mistress.

Among other practical matters, I felt free to raise the issue of postmortem access to the palazzo, pointing out that I might have trouble taking possession of the premises if someone were inside, to say nothing of the difficulties of scaling the high garden wall if no one were. Peggy considered the matter with the utmost seriousness and then took two characteristically simple measures. Addressing herself to the first eventuality, she let me prepare a brief "To Whom It May Concern" for her signature. Dated May 3, it said, "This is to certify that the Palazzo Venier dei Leoni and the art collection contained therein is the property of the Solomon R. Guggenheim Foundation in New York. It is therefore my wish that Mr. Thomas M. Messer, Director of the Guggenheim Museum in New York, or his deputy be admitted without delay to the above premises upon my death." Having considered the alternate situation, she simply handed me the one key that would open the garden gate as well as the palazzo portals.

Quotations in this essay are taken from correspondence in the Peggy Guggenheim Archives, Solomon R. Guggenheim Museum Archives.

May 24 — 31   1966.

Spent a pleasant exciting
week here, perfect hospitality
and many animated conversations

Lawrence Vail

5 Juin 66

délicieux de voir
Peggy   sans préméditation

Marcel Duchamp
Teeny

June 9   1966
Thank you so much
may I come again?
Henry Scrafella
Lois Bingham   Christopher Scott